Oct. 29, 2001

For Jane with all good
wishes —

Kathy

Friends Hold All Things in Common

FRIENDS HOLD ALL THINGS IN COMMON

Tradition, Intellectual
Property, and the
Adages of Erasmus

KATHY EDEN

Yale University Press   New Haven and London

Printed in the United States of America

ISBN: 0-300-08757-8 (cloth)
LOC Number: 068579

A catalogue record for this book is available from the
Library of Congress and the British Library.

The paper in this book meets the guidelines
for permanence and durability of the Committee
on Production Guidelines for Book Longevity of
the Council on Library Resources.

10 9 8 7 6 5 4 3 2 1

For my parents,
Theresa and Michael Eden

"Toto pectore" *(I.iv.26)*

CONTENTS

Acknowledgments

Thanks are due to the John Simon Guggenheim Memorial Foundation for a fellowship during the academic year 1998–99. Thanks are also due to Teodolinda Barolini, Mark Bauerlein, Caroline Bynum, Mary Carruthers, Cottrel Carson, Priscilla Ferguson, Robert Ferguson, Jennifer Fleischner, Moshe Gold, Anthony Grafton, Andrew Hacker, Sarah Hannah, Cole Harrop, John Hollander, Victoria Kahn, Richard Kuhns, Jasper Pirasteh, Peter Platt, Carey Ramos, Cathy Tempelsman, Wesley Trimpi, Ann Van Sant, and James Zetzel for lightening the task and leavening the argument.

"Ubi amici, ibi opes"
(I.iii.24)

Introduction

Responding in 1523 to a request from his friend John Botzheim, then Canon of Constance, to provide a catalogue of his
works, Erasmus recalls among many other things the unfortu-
nate events that occasioned his making a collection of Greek
and Roman proverbs — the project that secured his literary fame
throughout Europe and that has come down to us as the *Adages*.
Leaving England for the Continent by way of Dover in January
of 1500, Erasmus, as he remembers, found himself at odds with
an English customs officer. Having trusted the assurances of his
two English friends Thomas More and William Blount (Lord
Mountjoy) that customs regulations applied only to English cur-
rency, Erasmus had planned to leave the country with all of his
worldly wealth in foreign coins. To his surprise, the customs officer had other plans; and so Erasmus eventually found himself
back in Paris without any money, still smarting from what he
took to be a questionable confiscation of his property.

Despite the offense, Erasmus tells Botzheim more than
twenty years later, he resolved to overturn the expectations of a
watching world. Instead of penning his revenge, he chose to reaffirm his friendly feelings for the unwitting instrument of his
financial undoing (Ep. 1341A, Allen, I, 16–17; *CWE*, 9, 316):[1]

---

1. *Opus epistolarum Des. Erasmi Roterodami*, eds. P. S. Allen, H. M.
Allen, H. W. Garrod (Oxford, 1906–47), 11 vols., hereafter Allen; unless otherwise stated, all English translations of Erasmus from *Collected
Works of Erasmus* (Toronto, 1974–), hereafter *CWE*. Cf. Ep. 279, Allen, I,
537–39; *CWE*, 2, 260–61.

I had to prove to my friend Mountjoy that my feelings of friendship towards him had not changed in the least. And so I decided to publish something forthwith. Having nothing ready to hand, I accumulated at random from a few days' reading some sort of collection of adages (*sylvam aliquam adagiorum*), guessing that this book, such as it was, might find a welcome among those who wish to learn, at least for its utility. This I used as evidence that my friendship had not grown cold.

Thus dedicated to Mountjoy first as the *Collectanea* (1500) and thereafter as the *Adagiorum chiliades* or *Adages*, this "collection of adages" swelled gradually over the next quarter of a century to include more than 4000 proverbs.

Seeming almost as surprised by the success of his *Adages* as by the episode that engendered it, Erasmus also recounts for Botzheim how the collection grew (Allen, I, 17; *CWE*, 9, 316–17):

Moreover, as I saw that this work was so popular with keen students that it was clearly destined for a long life and was being published in competition by many printers, I enriched (*locupletavi*) it repeatedly as either leisure or a larger supply of books became available. The latest revision was published by Johann Froben in the year of our Lord 1523.

But the book did more than grow; it also spawned other literary projects. Among them were the *Parallels*, which, Erasmus explains to Botzheim, owed its existence to his "rereading a number of authors in order to enrich my *Adagia*" (*locupletandis Adagiis*) (Allen, I, 17; *CWE*, 9, 317).[2]

2. Erasmus confirms this plan in his dedicatory letter to Pieter Gillis for the *Parabolae* or *Parallels* (1514). See Ep. 312, Allen, II, 32–35; *CWE*,

Erasmus' recollection of the events surrounding the somewhat unlikely birth and growth of probably his most successful
literary brainchild foregrounds two key elements explored in the
pages that follow: friendship and property. As Margaret Mann
Phillips and others have noted, the *Adages* frequently considers
friendship not only as the explicit topic of more than a few ancient proverbs but also as the driving force behind this particular proverb-collector.[3] Even when Erasmus in the course of one
of his most famous adages, "The labors of Hercules" ("Herculei labores"), offers a somewhat different version of the circumstances motivating his collection — the express urgings of an im-
portunate Mountjoy instead of his own gracious reassurances to
an embarrassed Mountjoy — Erasmus attributes his motivation
to *amicitia* (III.i.1, LB, II, 715AB; *CWE,* 34, 179).[4]

Often identified with the theme of friendship, the *Adages* also

23, 130–34, where in describing the *Adagia* Erasmus uses language identi-
cal to that of 1523 (Allen, II, 33; *CWE,* 23, 130): "Of late, as I reread Aristotle, Pliny and Plutarch for the enrichment of my *Adagiorum Chiliades*
(*locupletandis Adagiorum Chiliadibus*), and cleared Annaeus Seneca of the
corruptions by which he was not so much disfigured as done away with
altogether, I noted down by the way these passages, to make an offering
for you which I knew would not be unwelcome."

See Natalie Zemon Davis, "Beyond the Market: Books as Gifts in
Sixteenth-Century France," *Transactions of the Royal Historical Society,* 33
(1983), 69–88.

3. See, for instance, T. C. Appelt, *Studies in the Contents and Sources
of Erasmus' "Adagia"* (Chicago, 1942), 43–44; Margaret Mann Phillips,
The "Adages" of Erasmus (Cambridge, 1964), 12–13, 111–12; John C. Olin,
"Erasmus' *Adagia* and More's *Utopia*" in *Miscellanea Moreana: Essays
for Germain Marc'hadour,* eds. Clare M. Murphy, Henry Gibaud, and
Mario A. DiCesare (Binghamton, N.Y., 1989), 127–36 and David Woot-
ton, "Friendship Portrayed: A New Account of *Utopia,*" *History Workshop
Journal* 45 (1998), 29–47.

4. *Desiderii Erasmi Roterodami Opera Omnia,* ed. J. Leclerc (Leiden,
1703–06), 10 vols., hereafter LB.

routinely reflects on the subject of property. As recorded in his letter to Botzheim, Erasmus' complaint concerning the unexpected loss of his money alerts us to the centrality of these reflections. So does his characterization of his revisions: he describes each new expansion as an effort to "enrich" his collection. As usual, Erasmus has chosen his words with a rhetorician's care, repeating the curious compound *locupletare* from *locus-plenus*, i.e. land-full or rich in real property.[5] This repetition is telling; for Erasmus specifically recalls offering his *Adages* to Mountjoy and his reading public as a treasury or storehouse of the accumulated wealth of Greek and Roman antiquity—in this case, not its material but its intellectual wealth: the wisdom of the ancients as part of the so-called classical tradition.[6] This wisdom, Erasmus claims in the *Prolegomena* or introduction to the *Adages* (1508), not only proves more durable than any piece of material property but is also most effectively transmitted from one generation to the next and from one culture to another in the form of proverbs (LB, II, 7F; *CWE*, 31, 16–17).

Not least valuable among this collection of proverbs is the one that Erasmus identifies as a good omen and places in first position (I.i.i, LB, II, 13F–14F; *CWE*, 31, 29–30): "Friends hold all things in common." Like Erasmus' account to Botzheim of the

5. Cf. Lewis and Short *s.v.* and see Cicero, *De re publica*, 2.16, discussed below.

6. So he writes to Mountjoy in the dedicatory letter to the 1508 Aldine edition (Ep. 211, Allen, I, 444; *CWE*, 2, 140–41), "Thus I included in my handbook adages drawn from a great many authors, to the number of more than three thousand two hundred; for why should we not count them up, like treasure?" In the dedicatory letter to the 1515 Froben edition (Ep. 269), Erasmus recounts his efforts to enrich (*locupletare*) his collection (Allen, I, 522, 525). In the following year, his good friend Budé refers to the *Adages* in Greek as "an important and imposing treasury of words (*logothēkēn*)" (Ep. 493, Allen, II, 392; *CWE*, 4, 139).

genesis of his proverb-collection, this particular proverb, as we will see in subsequent chapters, distills an ancient wisdom that recognizes the commonality between friendship and property. In the *Prolegomena*, in fact, Erasmus insists that whole volumes of philosophy merely amplify this common saying. "[A]nyone who deeply and diligently considers that remark of Pythagoras 'Between friends all is common,'" Erasmus insists, "will certainly find the whole of human happiness included in this brief saying. What other purpose has Plato in so many volumes except to urge a community of living, and the factor which creates it, namely friendship?" (LB, II, 6EF; *CWE*, 31, 15).

In keeping with the opening adage, my own account of the *Adages* will focus not only on these two ancient philosophers, Pythagoras and Plato, but on what they have in common, especially regarding friendship and property. These commonalities, I will argue, constitute no small part of the ancient philosophical tradition that Erasmus himself claims as his intellectual inheritance from the past. Not incidentally, these same commonalities also shape Erasmus' understanding of tradition itself—his understanding, that is, of how he stands in relation to the past. As we will see in some detail, Erasmus inherits a complex concept of tradition—one rooted in the legal transfer of property even while it is figured by his favorite philosophers as a sharing among friends. By drawing attention to this complex of traditions that informs the *Adages,* I hope to deepen our appreciation of Erasmus' understanding of tradition. For Erasmus would have agreed, I think, with those contemporary philosophers who hold that our relation to tradition—understood as everything that has come down to us from the past—is no trivial matter.[7]

7. See on this matter especially Hans-Georg Gadamer, *Truth and Method*, trans. Joel Weinsheimer and Donald G. Marshall (New York, 1989), esp. 277–307 and Gerald L. Bruns, "What is Tradition?" *New Lit-*

Without framing the problem in quite these terms, students of Renaissance humanism have recognized for some time that Erasmus often outspokenly distinguishes himself from his opponents on just this issue of relating to the past. Taking this recognition as its point of departure (and taking on something of the overall structure of an extended adage), my own study will gloss the proverbial saying about friendship and common property by focusing on Erasmus' encounter with so-called classical and Christian antiquity, and especially with its Platonic and Pythagorean strands. In these particular encounters with the past, as I hope to show, Erasmus discovers not only how he understands the relation between these two ancient traditions, classical and early Christian, but also (and no less significantly) how he understands himself as a reader of ancient texts to stand in relation to them. As even a casual look at his hermeneutics reveals, Erasmus reads the past as an activist committed both to practicing virtue and to furthering his practical commitment through his reading.[8]

Keenly aware of the force of tradition, Erasmus also brings to his reading of the past, as the letter to Botzheim attests, the special awareness of a professional writer. Indeed, Erasmus is arguably the first author to owe his successful career to both the new printing industry and the new intellectual property laws designed to safeguard its regulation.[9] If Erasmus derives from

---

erary History, 22 (1991), 1–21, who puts the fundamental hermeneutical question as "how we stand with respect to all that comes down to us from the past" (2).

8. On Erasmus' hermeneutics see my *Hermeneutics and the Rhetorical Tradition: Chapters in the Ancient Legacy and Its Humanist Reception* (New Haven, 1997), 64–78.

9. See Andrée Hayum, "Dürer's Portrait of Erasmus and the *Ars Typographorum,*" *Renaissance Quarterly,* 38 (1985), 650–87, esp. 662n: "Of course, the notion of plagiarism and intellectual property comes to the

antiquity his standing in regard to the past, in other words, he also realizes that the future for writers as well as readers will answer to changes brought about by these technological and legal innovations. No one in the early part of the sixteenth century has more incentive than Erasmus—preacher and practitioner of imitation—to wonder how changing attitudes toward "the right to copy" will affect the principles and practices of literary production. Collected to be used in common by both writers and readers, then, the *Adages*, as I will argue, not only credits antiquity with Renaissance humanism's understanding of tradition but also helps to set in motion the inevitable collision between a shared notion of a common tradition and the privately held interest in the written word that later centuries will call "intellectual property."

---

fore in a new way with the advent of printing; these were to be parallel concerns for Dürer and Erasmus throughout their careers."

I

What Do a Spoiled Egyptian, a Captive Woman, and a Pythagorean Have in Common?: Erasmus on Tradition

In one of his longest and most widely circulated adages, the "Sileni Alcibiadis," Erasmus rehearses his cultural program for cooperation between the classical and Christian traditions by situating Jesus in a long line of silenus-like figures: modest, even ridiculous on the outside; profoundly beautiful, even beatific on the inside. Beginning with Socrates, Erasmus traces this pedigree to include other ancient lovers of wisdom such as Antisthenes, Diogenes, Epictetus, the Hebrew prophets, and John the Baptist (III.iii.1; LB, II, 771B–772D; *CWE*, 34, 263–65). As he delineates this genealogy, he also briefly outlines its intellectual charter. And here, as in his most famous protreptic, the *Paraclesis*, this charter culminates in the controversial program of *philosophia Christi*.

Published the year after this adage and serving as introduction to his 1516 edition of the New Testament, the *Paraclesis* not only issues a call to the philosophy of Christ but does so with the help of some of the same pagan philosophers summoned in the adage. Echoing his essay on Alcibiades' figure of the silenus from Plato's *Symposium*, Erasmus asks in the biblical preface:[1]

---

1. *Paraclesis,* subtitled *Adhortatio ad Christianae philosophiae studium,* LB, V, 141F–142B; *Christian Humanism and the Reformation,* trans. John C. Olin (New York, 1965), 100–01. On *philosophia Christi* see Corne-

what else is the philosophy of Christ (*Christi phi-losophia*), which he himself calls a rebirth (*renascen-tiam*), than the restoration of human nature origi-nally well formed? By the same token, although no one has taught (*tradidit*) this more perfectly and more effectively than Christ, nevertheless one may find in the books of the pagans very much which does agree with His teaching. . . . What shall we say of this, that many—notably Socrates, Diogenes and Epictetus—have presented a good portion of His teaching?"

Not only do the teachings of some pagan philosophers coincide with Christian doctrine, but also their ancient wisdom, like passages of Scripture, can inspire exegetical activity conducive to pious living. So Erasmus concludes his discussion of Alcibia-

---

lis Augustijn, *Erasmus: His Life, Works, and Influence,* trans. J. C. Grayson (Toronto, 1991), 71–88 and 104–06; R. J. Schoeck, *Erasmus of Europe: The Prince of Humanists 1501–1536* (Edinburgh, 1993), 74–85; Preserved Smith, *Erasmus: A Study of His Life, Ideals and Place in History* (New York, 1923; rpt. 1962), 33–58 and James D. Tracy, *Erasmus of the Low Countries* (Berke-ley, 1996), 104–15 and 204–08. On the late antique uses of this term see J. Leclercq, "Pour l'histoire de l'expression 'philosophie chrétienne,'" *Mélanges de Science Religieuse,* 9 (1952), 221–26, and see Pierre Hadot, *Philosophy as a Way of Life,* trans. Michael Chase (Oxford, 1995), 129.

On the relation between the 1515 adage and the *Paraclesis,* see Margaret Mann Phillips, *The "Adages" of Erasmus,* 104 and "La 'Philosophia Christi' réfletée dans les 'Adages' d'Erasme," *Courants Religieux et Humanisme à la fin du XVe et au début du XVIe siècle* (Paris, 1959), 53–71. On the earliest stages of this Erasmian conflation of classical culture and Christianity, see Eugene F. Rice, Jr., "Erasmus and the Religious Tradition, 1495–1499," *Journal of the History of Ideas,* 11 (1950), 387–411.

For a different reading of the relation between *philosophia Christi* and the *studia humanitatis,* see Anthony Grafton and Lisa Jardine, *From Humanism to the Humanities* (Cambridge, Mass., 1986), esp. 136–49.

des' *sileni* by drawing the reader's attention both to the homiletic quality of this adage as a kind of *proverbi enarratio,* an exposition on the proverb, and to the overlapping roles of the *paroemio-graphus* and the *ecclesiastes*—the compiler of proverbs and the preacher (LB, II, 782B; *CWE,* 34, 281–82).

Closely associated with his philological efforts to improve both the Greek text of the New Testament and its Latin translation, Erasmus' program for cooperation between pagan and Christian antiquity encounters steady resistance within the Church.[2] At the same time, his sermon-like essays based on worldly learning, linked as they often were with the master-teacher of other-worldly wisdom, enjoyed enormous popularity, both individually and as part of the collection of roughly 4,000 proverbs called the *Adagiorum chiliades.* Indeed, the *Adages,* as advertised repeatedly by Erasmus himself, constitutes the treasury or storehouse of the intellectual wealth of classical antiquity collected for common use and thus one of his principal contributions to a cultural program for cooperation. Alongside such works as the *Antibarbarians* and the *Colloquies,* the *Adages* boldly proclaims Erasmus' allegiance to a position on the old and nagging question about what Athens has to do with Jerusalem, the Academy with the Church.

As Erasmus knew all too well, however, the answer to this question as first posed in the second century C.E. differed markedly from his own. In the frequently cited *De praescriptione hae-reticorum* (ch. 7), where Erasmus would have found the question in its original formulation, Tertullian bluntly rejects a motley

2. On Erasmus' opponents see his letter to Botzheim, Ep. 1341A, Allen, I, 22–29, *CWE,* 9, 326–39. And see also Erika Rummel, *Erasmus and His Catholic Critics* (Nieuwkoop, 1989), I, 15–61 and Tracy, *Erasmus of the Low Countries,* 183–203.

Christianity fashioned from the patchwork of Platonic, Stoic, and Peripatetic threads. Passionate in his dismissal of the Christian's need for even a passing acquaintance with—let alone a thorough grounding in—the classical tradition, Tertullian in this same work elucidates for these same Christians the very notion of tradition. And despite his wholesale rejection of things pagan, the jurisconsult-turned-Christian is keenly aware that tradition itself as a concept has deep roots in classical culture.[3]

For *traditio,* a term from Roman law, designates the most regular means for transferring the ownership of property. Compiler of Roman law before Justinian and Tertullian's near contemporary, Gaius distinguishes between *traditio* and other forms of conveyance such as *mancipatio,* identifying *traditio* as the customary informal transfer appropriate to things not manciple—what the Romans called *res nec mancipi.* As examples of such *res* or property Gaius cites gold, silver and clothing: "Thus when possession of clothes or gold or silver is delivered on account of a sale or gift or any other cause, the property passes at once, if the person who conveys is owner of them" (*Itaque si tibi vestem vel aurum vel argentum tradidero sive ex venditionis causa sive ex*

3. For the hypothesis that the jurisconsult and Christian were one and the same Tertullian see Timothy Barnes, *Tertullian* (Oxford, 1971), 22–29. Barnes rejects the hypothesis, emphasizing the sophistic over the juristic elements of Tertullian's writing.

On Tertullian's classicizing see Jerome, *Ep.* 70, discussed in more detail below (*Nicene and Post-Nicene Fathers,* VI, 151): "Can anything be more learned or more pointed than the style of Tertullian? His *Apology* and his books *Against the Gentiles* contain all the wisdom of the world?" Centuries later, in the *Antibarbarians,* Erasmus will make the same claim about Jerome and Augustine (*CWE,* 23, 55): "Augustine 'despised' heathen culture in this way, but only after becoming a prince of learning in this field. Jerome's 'contempt' for the writings of Cicero and Plato did not debar him from an excellent mastery of them, and he used them continuously."

donationis sive quavis alia ex causa, statim tua fit ea res, si modo ego eius dominus sim).[4]

Adapting throughout his treatise the specialized language of Roman law, beginning with the *praescriptio* of his title, Tertullian defends the teachings handed down by the apostles as the property of all true Christians. Sometimes he refers to this handing down as *traditio apostolorum* (21), and at other times as *traditiones Christianae* (19; cf. 28). And in keeping with his forensic terminology, he undertakes to preempt controversy with heretical opponents over doctrinal issues on the grounds that they can lay no claim to the scripture that would either substantiate or undermine their positions. In stark contrast to true Christians, Tertullian asserts with lawyerly logic, these heretics cannot use what they do not own (37):[5]

---

4. *Gai Institutiones or Institutes of Roman Law by Gaius,* trans. Edward Poste and Rev. E. A. Whittuck (London, 1904), II, 20, p. 134. And see 133–39, which concludes: "In Justinian's time Tradition had entirely superseded the civil titles of surrender before the magistrate and mancipation: the ancient distinction between res mancipi and res nec mancipi being no longer in existence." On *traditio* as a legal term see also Yves M.-J. Congar, *Tradition and Traditions* (New York, 1967), 244–52. For its continuity in the specialized language of English law, see for instance Thomas Hobbes, *Leviathan,* eds. Richard E. Flathman and David Johnston (New York, 1997), ch. 14, p. 74: "The mutuall transferring of Right, is that which men call Contract. There is difference, between transferring of Right to the Thing; and transferring, or tradition, that is, delivery of the Thing it selfe. For the Thing may be delivered together with the Translation of the Right; as in buying and selling with ready mony; or exchange of goods, or lands; and it may be delivered some time after."

5. *De praescriptione haereticorum,* ed. T. Herbert Bindley (Oxford, 1893); *The Prescription against Heretics* in *The Ante-Nicene Fathers,* eds. Alexander Roberts and James Donaldson (Edinburgh, 1884; rpt. Grand Rapids, Michigan, 1993), III, 243–65. On the legal sense of *praescriptio,* see Bindley, 4–5 and *Gai institutiones,* s.v. See also Albert C. Outler, "The Sense of Tradition in the Ante-Nicene Church," *The Heritage of Christian*

Thus, not being Christians, they have acquired no right to the Christian Scriptures (*Christianarum litterarum*); and it may be very fairly said to them, "Who are you? When and whence did you come? As you are none of mine, what have you to do with that which is mine? . . . This is my property (*Mea est possessio*). Why are you, the rest, sowing and feeding here at your own pleasure? This (I say) is my property. I have long possessed it; I possessed it before you. I hold sure title-deeds (*origines firmas*) from the original owners themselves (*ab ipsis auctoribus*), to whom the estate (*res*) belonged. I am the heir of the apostles (*heres apostolorum*). Just as they carefully prepared their will and testament (*testamento*), and committed it to a trust (*fidei commiserunt*), and adjured (the trustees to be faithful to their charge), even so do I hold it. As for you, they have, it is certain, always held you as disinherited (*exheredaverunt*), and rejected (*abdicaverunt*) you as strangers —as enemies."

Tertullian's case against his adversaries, in other words, depends on the extension of some of the most basic principles of Roman property law to this "intellectual property" of all true Christians. For it is fully in keeping with this law, he insists, that

---

Thought: Essays in Honor of Robert Lowry Calhoun, eds. Robert E. Cushman and Egil Grislis (New York, 1965), 18–21. For Augustine's similar argument against the Manicheans, see Georges Florovsky, "The Function of Tradition in the Ancient Church," *The Greek Orthodox Theological Review,* 9 (1963–64), 199–200.

In 1521, Beatus Rhenanus, Erasmus' friend and biographer, published the first edition of Tertullian's works. See Erasmus' letter to Botzheim, Ep. 1341A, Allen, I, 15; *CWE,* 9, 313–14.

only those to whom property has been rightfully handed over or traditioned—in Latin, *tradita*—can exercise the privileges of ownership. They alone are heirs of the apostles.

In its exploitation of the broad and deep influence of ancient legal theory and practice on late antique culture, Tertullian's treatment of tradition, and more precisely of apostolic tradition, shares many of its assumptions with other early fathers of the Church, Greek as well as Latin.[6] Concerning his position on the so-called classical tradition, on the other hand, Tertullian parts company with some from well within ecclesiastical ranks.

Origen, for instance, in his influential "Letter to Gregory," affirms the usefulness of Greek philosophy as a propaedeutic, a preparation, for the study of Scripture (1) and adduces in this regard scriptural evidence from Exodus (i.e., 3:22, 12:35–36). "Perhaps something of this kind," Origen writes (2), "is shadowed forth in what is written in Exodus from the mouth of God, that the children of Israel were commanded to ask from their neighbors, and those who dwelt with them, vessels of silver and gold, and raiment, in order that, by spoiling the Egyptians, they might have material for the preparation of the things which pertained to the service of God."[7] For while the faint-hearted may

6. See Congar, 23–85.
7. "A Letter from Origen to Gregory," *The Ante-Nicene Fathers*, IV, 393–4. See also Henri de Lubac, *Exégèse médiévale* (Paris, 1959), I, 290–304 and André Godin, *Erasme Lecteur d'Origène* (Geneva, 1982), 18 and "The *Enchiridion Militis Christiani:* The Modes of an Origenian Appropriation," *Erasmus of Rotterdam Society Yearbook*, 2 (1982), 47–79.

On some other early Christian uses of both the *spoliatio Aegyptiorum* and the *mulier captiva*, see Mary Carruthers, *The Craft of Thought: Meditation, Rhetoric, and the Making of Images 400–1200* (Cambridge, 1998), 125–30; and see Carol E. Quillen, "Plundering the Egyptians: Petrarch and Augustine's *De doctrina christiana*," *Reading and Wisdom: The De doctrina of Augustine in the Middle Ages*, ed. Edward D. English (Notre Dame, 1995), 153–71.

admittedly use foreign wealth in the service of idolatry to craft a golden calf, the steadfast can use the same riches for vessels of holiness: the ark, the seat of mercy, and the sacred coffer for the bread of angels (2).

Origen's exegesis of the so-called *spoliatio Aegyptiorum* serves as a powerful defense for the proper use of classical culture, in spite of routine attacks on his alleged heterodoxy. And it is worth noting that here too, in the figure from Exodus (where the articles taken correspond exactly to those traditioned in the *Institutes* of Gaius), Origen understands the intellectual tradition under consideration in terms of property: not in this case property handed over to a rightful heir according to legal procedure, like the apostolic tradition in the possession of faithful Christians, but property seized from an enemy as an act of aggression. Basil of Caesarea and his friend Gregory Nazianzus help to assure the widespread transmission of Origen's exegesis in their once well-known *Philocalia*.[8] So does Augustine, in his still enormously popular treatise on what the Christian should know: the *De doctrina christiana*.[9]

Echoing Origen's defense of classical learning as an aid to understanding scripture, the second book of the *De doctrina* ends with the same figure of the Israelites' despoiling the Egyptians (2.40.60; cf. 2.41.62–2.42.63):[10]

8. On the *Philocalia* see Philip Rousseau, *Basil of Caesarea* (Berkeley, 1994), 11–14, 82–84.

9. Erasmus' ten-volume edition of Augustine's *Opera Omnia* is published in 1528; his edition of Origen, completed by Beatus Rhenanus after Erasmus' death, in 1536. On the edition of Augustine, see *CWE*, 9, 349–50. For his work on the early Fathers, see Augustijn, 100. For his familiarity with Origen, see André Godin, *Erasme Lecteur d'Origène* and Tracy, *Erasmus of the Low Countries*, 32–35. On the early reception of Origen and the controversies surrounding his writings see Elizabeth Clark, *The Origenist Controversy* (Princeton, 1992).

10. *Oeuvres de Saint Augustin,* eds. G. Combès and J. Farges (Paris,

If those who are called philosophers, especially the Platonists, have said things which are indeed true and are well accommodated to our faith, they should not be feared; rather what they have said should be taken from them (*vindicanda*) as from unjust possessors (*injustis possessoribus*) and converted to our use. Just as the Egyptians had not only idols and grave burdens which the people of Israel detested and avoided, so also they had vases and ornaments of gold and silver and clothing which the Israelites took with them (*vindicavit*) secretly when they fled, as if to put them to better use. They did not do this on their own authority (*auctoritate propria*) but as God's commandment, while the Egyptians unwittingly supplied them with things which they themselves did not use well.

As argued by the teacher of rhetoric steeped in classical culture including the law, the Christians' legal claim or *vindicatio* to pagan property—here intellectual property—rests on God's legal authority or *auctoritas* as original owner to take away from unjust possessors what He has given them and to bestow it elsewhere. For proof Augustine offers precedent: God's authorizing the Israelites' claim to Egyptian property.[11]

1949), XI, 168–541; *On Christian Doctrine,* trans. D. W. Robertson (Indianapolis, 1958).

11. See the note on this figure in *Oeuvres de Saint Augustin,* XI, 582–84. Augustine uses this same figure in regard to the literary property of the Platonists in his *Confessions* (7.9.15).

On *vindicatio* as a legal term see *Gai institutiones,* 443 and Alan Watson, *The Law of Property in the Later Roman Republic* (Oxford, 1968), 96–104. On *auctoritas,* see Watson, *Rome of the XII Tables: Persons and Property* (Princeton, 1975), 141–43, 151–52 and on *auctor,* see David Daube, "Fashions and Idiosyncracies in the Exposition of the Roman Law of

While borrowing the specialized terminology of the law courts—terms such as *auctoritas, vindicatio,* and *possessiv*—Augustine builds an admittedly rhetorical rather than a legal case for the Christian's right to the classical, especially the Platonic, tradition. In doing so, he creates in turn his own invaluable precedent for subsequent rhetoricians caught in later debates over the propriety or impropriety of using the intellectual wealth of so-called classical antiquity in the service of Christianity. As I have already noted, one such rhetorician so caught is Erasmus. Proclaiming himself the rightful heir of both early Christian and classical traditions, Erasmus reinvests his Augustinian legacy in order to advance his claim, as did Augustine before him, to the ancient philosophical, especially Platonic, tradition.

It is particularly appropriate, therefore, that one of Erasmus' most significant early works in this effort, the *Antibarbarians,* mounts its attack on the enemies of classical learning in the form of a Platonic dialogue on the model of the *Republic* and *Phaedrus.*[12] Its principal speaker, Jacob Batt, argues his case with the

---

Property," *Theories of Property: Aristotle to the Present,* eds. Anthony Parel and Thomas Flanagan (Waterloo, Ontario, 1979), 41–42. And on *possessio,* see *Gai institutiones,* s.v.

12. In the letter to Botzheim (1523), Erasmus refers to the *Antibarbari* as a declamation, a work of his youth (*CWE,* 9, 321) and as unfinished (*CWE,* 9, 346–47). See James D. Tracy, "Against the 'Barbarians': The Young Erasmus and His Humanist Contemporaries," *Sixteenth-Century Journal,* 11 (1980), 3–22 and *Erasmus of the Low Countries,* 24–26. On its dependence on the *Republic* and *Phaedrus,* see the introductory letter of 1520 (Ep. 1110), *CWE,* 23, 16 and *Antibarbari, CWE,* 23, 39–40 and 119.

On its dependence on the *De doctrina* see Charles Béné, *Erasme et Saint Augustin* (Geneva, 1969), 59–95; on its use of the *spoliatio Aegyptiorum,* see Marjorie O'Rourke Boyle, *Christening Pagan Mysteries: Erasmus in Pursuit of Wisdom* (Toronto, 1981), 3–25, esp. 16–17 and Ernst-Wilhelm Kohls, *Die Theologie des Erasmus* (Basel, 1966), I, 35–37 and II, 55–56.

help of two unimpeachable witnesses: one is Jerome, and more precisely, Jerome's exegesis in his seventieth letter of the *mulier captiva*, the "captive woman" of Deuteronomy 21; the other is Augustine—in particular, his exegesis from the end of the second book of the *De doctrina* on spoiling the Egyptians. Both proof-texts, not coincidentally, figure the classical tradition as property appropriated from an enemy.[13]

Defending himself in a letter to the orator Magnus (*Ep.* 70) against the charge of muddying his Christian polemics with evidence from classical literature, Jerome adduces the testimony not only of Moses and the prophets, who made good use of gentile learning, but also Paul. In his own battle against the Greek intellectuals of his day (i.e., Acts 17:22–31), Jerome argues, Paul followed both the example of David and the injunction of Deuteronomy (70.2):[14]

13. Although this dialogue, like Plato's *Republic* and *Phaedrus*, explores the notion of friendship, it figures the traditionary relation as one between enemies. For the role of friendship in the Erasmian dialogue, see, for instance, *CWE*, 23, 19–21. For Erasmus' friendship with Batt, see Ep. 159, Allen, I, 366–67.

Among the schools of ancient philosophy, the *Enchiridion* favors the Academy (*CWE*, 66, 33): "Of the philosophers I should recommend the Platonists because in much of their thinking as well as in their mode of expression they are the closest to the spirit of the prophets and the gospel."

See also Edmund Campion, "Defences of Classical Learning in St. Augustine's *De Doctrina Christiana* and Erasmus's *Antibarbari*," *History of European Ideas*, 4 (1983), 467–72.

14. *CSEL*, 54, 700–08; trans. *Nicene and Post-Nicene Fathers*, 6, 149–51. See, in addition, Johannes Quasten, "A Pythagorean Idea in Jerome," *American Journal of Philology*, 63 (1942), 207–15, where Quasten not only links Jerome's distinction between woolen and linen garments before and after baptism with Pythagorean (and Orphic) ritual but refers to the custom of removing nails and hair as another form of bodily refuse in terms suggestive for the rituals performed on the *mulier captiva* to make her

the leader of the Christian army, the matchless orator pleading the cause of Christ, turns round a chance inscription to make it into an argument of faith. He had learnt from the true David to seize the sword out of the hands of the enemy, and cut off the arrogant head of Goliath with his own blade. He had read in Deuteronomy the command delivered by the voice of the Lord, that the captive woman should have her head and eyebrows shaved, all the hair and nails of her body cut off, and thus she should be taken to wife.

Whether seizing an enemy's weapons or his women, in other words, the reader of *scriptura* is encouraged to turn that enemy's property to good use. And what Paul has learned from reading Hebrew Scripture, Jerome has learned by his own admission from reading Paul.

On the other hand, Jerome does not here admit to reading Origen, who had much more explicitly than Paul turned the figure of the captive woman—as he had that of spoiling the Egyptians—to good use in justifying the Christian's claim to the intellectual, especially literary, property of classical antiquity.[15] In a homily on Leviticus (VII, 6), Origen digresses from an exegesis of the prescriptions concerning animals suitable for eating (11:3-7) to one concerning captive women suitable for

---

suitable for marrying. For Jerome's admitting to reading Pythagoras, see his letter to Pammachius and Oceanus (84.6). For Erasmus' edition of Jerome's Letter to Magnus see *CWE*, 61, 201–06.

15. Jerome cites Origen in this same letter (3–4) as precedent for the godly use of secular learning. On Jerome's use of Origen see Elizabeth Clark, *The Origenist Controversy*, 121–51. And see R. P. C. Hanson, *Origen's Doctrine of Tradition* (London, 1954), who does not discuss either the *mulier captiva* or the *spoliatio Aegyptiorum*.

marrying—a digression motivated, he explains, by attention in each case to the condition of the fingernails or hoofs: *onuches* in Greek and *ungulae* in Latin (VII, 6, 75–77). Earlier in the same chapter he had already introduced those ancient philosophers— namely the Platonists and Pythagoreans—who, while lacking faith, taught both the immortality of the soul and its divine reward or punishment in afterlife; there he compared them to animals who have cloven hoofs but do not chew their cud. He now continues, by way of the figure of the captive woman, to explain that whatever wisdom the Christian reads in the teachings of these philosophers must, like a beautiful woman seized from the enemy, undergo purification before being embraced as a wife.

What Jerome has learned from reading Paul and presumably Origen, Batt in turn has learned from reading Jerome (LB, X, 1729DF; *CWE*, 23, 92). All of these readers, moreover, apply this figure of an enemy's property to their intellectual or, more precisely, their literary property. Just as Paul in the passage from Acts interprets the pagan inscription to serve his Christian preaching on the Areopagus and Origen adduces what it is lawful to eat in arguing about what it is lawful to read, so Jerome wonders aloud in his letter to Magnus if it is "surprising that I too, admiring the fairness of her form and the grace of her eloquence, desire to make that secular wisdom which is my captive and my handmaid, a matron of true Israel" (70.2).

In due time Batt, openly following Jerome, pleads a similar case for using the classical literary tradition. "Is everything which came out of the heathen world," Batt asks, "always to be bad, and forbidden to Christians? So we are not allowed to take over (*usurpare*) anything discovered by the pagans unless we cease forthwith to be Christians?" (LB, X, 1710F; *CWE*, 23, 56). Here as hereafter in the reading of Jerome's letter, Batt both understands tradition in legal terms and figures the traditionary relation between pagan antiquity and Christianity as an extra-legal, even hostile, appropriation: in this case, a *usurpatio*.

Erasmus' other significant early work in this effort is the *Enchiridion Militis Christiani*, the so-called *Handbook of the Christian Soldier*. As the title itself sets in relief, the relation here of the Christian to the world, including worldly learning, is adversarial. Accordingly, Erasmus not only figures the traditionary relation as one between enemies, but he adduces the same witnesses that made Batt's case in the *Antibarbarians*. In a chapter entitled *De armis militiae Christianae*—"The Armour of the Christian Militia"—he once again calls on Jerome to testify "concerning his beloved female captive" (LB, V, 7D; *CWE*, 66, 33; cf. LB, V, 8AB; *CWE*, 66, 34); Erasmus then reinforces Jerome's testimony with Augustine's from the *De doctrina*, where the Church Father praises his own predecessor Cyprian "because he enriched the temple of the Lord with Egyptian spoils" (*CWE*, 66, 33).[16]

16. Although the *mulier captiva*, like the *spoliatio Aegyptiorum*, looks back to Origen, Godin concludes that "Jérôme avait emprunté cette allégorie à Origène mais Erasme l'ignorait même en composant l'*Enchiridion*" (*Erasme Lecteur d'Origène*, 17). And see Godin, "The *Enchiridion Militis Christiani*: The Modes of an Origenian Appropriation," *Erasmus of Rotterdam Society Yearbook*, 2 (1982), 47–79. Especially intriguing in regard to Erasmus' use of the *mulier captiva* is Godin's conclusion that (75), "About half (15 out of 35) of these cryptic citations are found in the second chapter ('The Weapons of the Christian Soldier') whose importance is decisive for the architecture of the work. In my view, this section of the *Enchiridion* presents the all-but-perfect model of the Erasmian technique by way of borrowing. This first pronouncement of the 'gnesia pietas' and the 'vera theologia'—the conjunction of which forms what he will call, after 1516, the 'philosophia Christi'—(with data drawn almost exclusively from the corpus of the Origenian *Homilies on Exodus, Josuah*, and *Numbers*) fits nicely into the exposition of the Erasmian program, while structuring and embellishing it."

In addition, see James D. Tracy, "The 1489 and 1494 Versions of Eras-

Cited only very briefly in the *Enchiridion* to justify reading classical literature as a propaedeutic to reading Scripture, the Augustinian passage receives much fuller treatment in the *Antibarbarians*. Indeed, Erasmus has Batt rehearse it at some length. "I wish I could give you the exact words of what follows," Batt admits (LB, X, 1732BE; *CWE*, 23, 97):

> a charming passage about the household goods of the Egyptians (*de Aegyptia supellectile*), but nevertheless I will give a faithful account of it: we read in Exodus, [Augustine] says, that when the Hebrews were secretly preparing to fly under their leader Moses from their servitude in Egypt, each took from his obliging neighbor all sorts of household goods (*plurimam omnis generis supellectilem*), an immense amount of rings, clothes, and vessels, and, having spoiled the Egyptians, they departed, secretly. As we know that this flight, this theft (*furtum*), was done with the sanction of God (*Deo auctore*), we may take it that there is a significance here: that divine providence was acting in consideration for the timidity of some people who would have been frightened to spoil the Egyptians, that is to take over the wisdom of the heathen, unless they had such an example of this very thing, such a commander, such a leader. To come out of Egypt is to

---

mus' Antibarbarorum Liber," *Humanistica Lovaniensia*, 20 (1971), 81–120, esp. 94: "But the 1494/5 *Antibarbari*, representing new experience of the world, new reading, and new friends like James Batt, remains nonetheless a watershed in his intellectual development. Refusing any longer to regard the world primarily as a source of temptation, he took up his lifelong task of working for a reform of Christian society through a reform of education."

leave behind heathen superstition and be converted to the Christian religion. To take away the wealth (*opes*) of Egypt is to transfer (*transfert*) heathen literature to the adornment and use of our faith. The barbarians will perhaps make fun of the interpreter, and they would be right, if I were not putting forward Augustine's interpretation, not mine. For just as the Hebrews, he says, in old days seized whatever they judged would be harmful, or useless, or unhallowed, so it behoves us to leave to the heathen their vices, superstitions, lusts, desires—these I say, are to be left to their owners (*apud dominos*). But if there is among them any gold of wisdom, any silver of speech, and furniture of good learning (*supellex bonarum litterarum*), we should pack up all that baggage and turn it to our own use, never fearing to be accused of thieving (*furti*), but rather venturing to hope for reward and praise for the finest of deeds.

Introducing the passage from the *De doctrina* as a *bona fides* rendering rather than a direct quotation, Erasmus has Batt not only paraphrase but amplify Augustine's words. Indeed, he even has Batt sharpen the legalistic coloring of the Augustinian original, justifying more fully what might be condemned as the illegal transfer of property by theft (*furtum*). Granting ownership or *dominium* to the Egyptians, Batt, like Augustine, nevertheless gives the ultimate legal title or *auctoritas* to God. Furthermore, Erasmus has Batt repeat a key term—*supellex*—that does not occur in the Augustinian argument but does figure prominently in discussions of Roman property.[17] By its third and last occur-

17. On *supellex* see Cicero, *Topica* 5.27 and Alan Watson, *Roman Private Law around 200 B.C.* (Edinburgh, 1971), 113–14. On *epipla*, the

rence in this passage, *supellex* characterizes specifically intellectual or literary property: *supellex bonarum litterarum,* here translated as the "furniture of good learning" but reasonably understood as "valuable literary property."

Figuring the classical literary tradition as Egyptian property, especially "furniture" or movables, clearly appealed to Erasmus; for he also uses this figure in an early letter (1496) to Hendrik van Bergen, Bishop of Cambrai, to characterize the classicizing poetry of his dear friend, Willem Hermans of Gouda, a young poet familiar to Erasmus' readers through his key role in the *Antibarbari.*[18] Soliciting the bishop's help, Erasmus expresses his wish in this letter to publish a book of his friend's odes (*Ep.* 49, Allen, I, 160–64, *CWE,* 1, 99–105). To its credit, Erasmus argues, Hermans' poetry combines Christian themes with classical forms; it uses Egyptian furnishings, *supellex Aegyptia,* while avoiding "the appropriation of Egypt in its entirety" (*Neque improbaverim Aegyptiam adhiberi supellectilem; verum totam Aegyptum transferri non placet.*) (Allen, I, 163; *CWE,* 1, 103).

As we have seen thus far, Erasmus inherits from patristic tradition not only particular biblical passages for defending the Christian's right to classical literary culture but also a notion of tradition itself modeled on the legal transfer of property, material property. According to this legal model, the material of various traditions, like private property, rightfully belongs to some and not to others. As the exegetical tradition of the *spoliatio Aegyptiorum*—bolstered by that of the *mulier captiva*—sets in high relief, the so-called classical tradition belongs to Christians

---

Greek equivalent of *supellex,* see Aristotle, *Politics,* 2.14.12 and *Rhetoric,* 1.5.7.

18. See the opening of the *Antibarbari,* where Erasmus refers to Hermans as "the one among my contemporaries who was much the dearest to me" (*CWE,* 28, 19).

through a hostile act of appropriation—a transfer of property between enemies. In some of his later works, as the remainder of this chapter will show, Erasmus skillfully reconfigures this traditionary relation, substituting for the appropriated property of enemies the shared property of friends.

A fine example—maybe the finest—of this substitution is the *Adages*. Making available for common use the collected intellectual wealth of the classical tradition, the *Adages* begins with a proverb about friendship, and not only about friendship but about the common ownership of property among friends. Erasmus, that is, inaugurates the entire collection of over 4,000 proverbs with the often-cited Greek adage "Koina ta tōn philōn," rendered into Latin as "Amicorum communia omnia" and into English as "Friends hold all things in common." In fact, Erasmus has strategically moved this adage from somewhere in the middle of his earliest assembly of adages called the *Collectanea* (1500) to initial position in the fuller *Adagiorum chiliades* (1508), thereby establishing the proverb's status as programmatic for the collection as a whole.

In keeping with this program, moreover, Erasmus revises the opening adage for the 1508 edition to feature Plato and Pythagoras: the ancient Italian philosopher as the founding father of pagan communalism as well as of the saying itself, the Athenian philosopher as Pythagoras' most persuasive disciple, and both because their teachings accord with the teachings of Christ.[19] So in his discussion of this proverb Erasmus expresses puzzlement

19. For Jerome's early attention to Plato and Pythagoras and for the same reasons, see Ep. 84.6, which addresses his reading of Origen (*Nicene and Post-Nicene Fathers,* VI, 178): "Now suppose for a moment that in my youth I went astray and that, trained as I was in the schools of heathen philosophy, I was ignorant, in the beginning of my faith, of the dogmas of Christianity, and fancied that what I had read in Pythagoras and Plato and Empedocles was also contained in the writings of the apostles."

at how "Christians dislike this common ownership of Plato's, how in fact they cast stones at it, although nothing was ever said by a pagan philosopher which comes closer to the mind of Christ" (LB, II, 14C; *CWE*, 31, 30). And so he concludes the adage by applauding Pythagoras, who "instituted a kind of sharing of life and property in this way, the very thing Christ wants to happen among Christians" (LB, II, 14E; *CWE*, 31, 30).

In the opening adage, then, Erasmus underscores the commonalities found in Pythagorean, Platonic, and Christian values. This is not, however, his readers' first encounter with this theme. For Erasmus has already drawn their attention to it in the longer *Prolegomena* that, complementing the first adage's relocation, replaces the briefer *Praefatio* that had introduced the earlier *Collectanea*. In this expanded introduction of 1508, moreover, Erasmus introduces the commonalities found in Pythagoras, Plato, and Christ in order to argue more generally for the close alliance between proverbs and philosophy. Both the founder of the Academy and the Redeemer, he insists, practiced proverbial statement. Plato did so with such skill that he deserves the singular title *paroimiōdesteros* (LB, II, 5C), "master of proverbs," while Christ is said to take "particular delight in this way of speaking" (LB, II, 5E; *CWE*, 31, 13). Indeed, Erasmus not only aligns these two philosophers, Plato and Christ, with proverbial statement, but he here characterizes the proverb itself in ways that anticipate the characterization of these same philosophers in the "Sileni Alcibiadis." Shadowing forth the silenus-like figures of the later adage, especially such figures as Socrates and Christ, Erasmus describes proverbs as "things which are most important and even divine . . . expressed in . . . a trivial and seemingly almost ridiculous nature" (LB, II, 6D; *CWE*, 31, 14).

To support this argument in the introduction for the alliance between proverbial expression and philosophy, Erasmus cites two proverbs in particular. One is our Pythagorean adage on friendship and common property; the other is the Hesiodic proverb "The half is more than the whole" (LB, II, 6D-7A; *CWE*, 31, 14-15). Erasmus couples the Hesiodic and Pythagorean adages, it is worth noting, not only because both express values commonly held by Plato and Christ but also because both formulate these values in terms of property. Accordingly, Erasmus first identifies the Hesiodic adage in the *Prolegomena* as the original, densely compressed wisdom of a more remote antiquity subsequently expanded by Plato in the *Gorgias* and the *Republic*. This expansion, he suggests, generates in turn the well-known Platonic paradox that it is better to receive an injury than to inflict one. "What doctrine," Erasmus asks, "was ever produced by the philosophers more salutary as a principle of life or closer to the Christian religion?" (LB, II, 6E; *CWE*, 31,14). In this passage, moreover, Erasmus identifies Platonic injury more narrowly with fraud—an injury specifically related to the misappropriation of property (LB, II, 6E; *CWE*, 31, 14-15; cf. LB, II, 366A; *CWE*, 32, 230).

Then, in his fuller exposition of this adage later in the collection (I.ix.95; LB, II, 364C-366B; *CWE*, 32, 228-31), Erasmus reinforces its applicability to conflicts over property by supplementing his earlier reading with the Platonic opposition between *isotēs* and *pleonexia*—that is, between taking one's fair share and taking more than one's share (LB, II, 364D). Not only Plato, but before him Hesiod and Pittacus and after him "Suidas" apply this adage to circumstances concerning the fair and unfair disposition of property. According to Diogenes Laertius (1.75), Pittacus accepted only half the land allotted to him by the people of Mytilene on the authority of this proverb, whereas according to Hesiod (*Works and Days*, 37-41), his own brother Perseus defied this same proverbial wisdom and took more than his fair share of their father's inheritance (LB, II, 364EF). Finally, Erasmus has "Suidas" corroborate this earlier testimony by telling his own tale (LB, II, 365BC; *CWE*, 32, 229):

> Once upon a time there were two brothers, one of whom died, leaving the other by his will as a guardian of his son, who was still a minor, and trustee of his estate. However the brother was no better than the common run of men—he cared more for coin than his duty to his family, tried to seize the son's property, and in the process lost both it and his own. Then, when he asked for sympathy in hopes of recovering his position, the answer took the form: "Fool, he has never learnt how much more half than whole is." And so kings take half, and tyrants take everything.

In reading this proverb in light of the notion of fairness or equality, especially as it pertains to matters of property, Erasmus is following his ancient sources. Like these same sources, in his fuller exposition of this adage, he also associates equality with fairness as the basis of friendship, and thus with Pythagoras as the philosopher of friendship (LB, II, 365D; *CWE*, 32, 230). This association inevitably draws the reader's attention back to the *Prolegomena*'s brief mention of this adage, where, as we have seen, it keeps company with the Pythagorean adage, which is even more explicitly about friendship and property—common property.

With both the 1508 introduction and the opening adage, then, Erasmus initiates the larger claim of the work as a whole. Nearly a decade before the *Paraclesis* and the "Sileni Alcibiadis," that is to say, the first edition of the *Adagiorum chiliades* inaugurates the very program of cooperation that Erasmus will later come to call *philosophia Christi*. Indeed, the first adage, as characterized in the revised introduction, is paradigmatically silenus-like, housing a divine interior within a modest exterior an ocean of philosophy or theology (*oceanus philosophiae vel theologiae magis*) (LB, II, 7B) expressed in so few words. Anyone considering Pythagoras' remark, as we have already seen above, will find the teachings not only of Plato but also of Christ (LB, II, 6F-7A; *CWE*, 31, 15):

> What other purpose had Christ, the prince of our religion? One precept and one alone He gave (*tradidit*) to the world, and that was love (*caritatis*); on that alone, He taught, hang all the law and the prophets. Or what else does love (*caritas*) teach us, except that all things should be common to all (*aut omnium omnia sint communia*)?

Partners in rejecting individual ownership of private property, Plato, Pythagoras, and Christ all share a corresponding intellectual tradition that endorses community rooted in likemindedness. Without necessarily sharing their conviction about material property,[20] Erasmus does make a compelling case on the basis of this proverb for his and every other Christian's proprietary right to the classical tradition. On this crucial issue, in fact, he gradually distances himself from his more openly acknowledged patristic sources. Whereas they feel compelled to defend Christianity against the charge of appropriating an enemy's property, he concentrates instead on promoting the philosophical commonalities between two mutually enriching traditions.

20. In 1526, possibly in response to the Anabaptists, Erasmus adds a reference to Aristotle's critique of common property from book 2 of the *Politics* (LB, II, 14CD; *CWE*, 31, 30). For Erasmus' influence on Anabaptism see Abraham Friesen, *Erasmus, the Anabaptists and the Great Commission* (Grand Rapids, 1998).

So in the *De doctrina* Augustine only grudgingly admits Pythagoras' claim to wisdom through his debt to Hebrew scripture (2.28.43). As early as the *Antibarbarians,* in contrast, Erasmus has Batt willingly grant Pythagoras' authority as the first philosopher, even while he continues to figure the classical tradition as the appropriated property of an enemy (*CWE*, 23, 68–69).[21] It would be a mistake, however, to assume that Erasmus relies on the biblical figure because he has yet to discover the Pythagorean adage. For in the same early letter to Hendrik van Bergen cited above, Erasmus playfully refers to his right to publish Hermans' poetry without the author's express consent—that is, he establishes his right to this particular piece of literary property—on the grounds of the old adage. "I will urge that it is illegal to bring a charge of theft against me," he asserts as early as 1496, "since, as Pythagoras has truly remarked, friends have all things in common" (*Dicam preter ius me furti accusari, quod [ut vere a Pytagora dictum est] amicorum inter se communia sint omnia*) (Allen, I, 162; *CWE*, 1, 103).

With the publication of the first edition of the *Adages* in 1508, on the other hand, the reader finds Erasmus putting increased pressure on this claim of friendship—pressure that begins with the revised introduction or *Prolegomena* and continues with the opening adage. Under its proverbial protection, as we have already seen in the 1515 adage "Sileni Alcibiadis," Erasmus will go on to defend Christ's equal ownership of the title of philoso-

---

21. See Boyle, *Christening Pagan Mysteries,* 12–14 and 55–58, which concludes, "*Adagia,* as the Moria, represents more than 'despoiling the Egyptians,' as had the Hebrews who stole their gold and proverbs. It appreciatively integrates pagan wisdom with the Christian economy, in agreement with the theological conviction voiced in *Antibarbari.*" See also M. M. Phillips, *The "Adages" of Erasmus* (Cambridge, 1964), 85–86.

pher—a title he shares quite amicably with Plato and Pythagoras.[22] Far from depriving Christians of what rightfully belongs to them, then, *philosophia Christi* increases their common intellectual store by supplementing the apostolic tradition with what Erasmus (as we will see in chapter 6) will call in yet another adage of the 1508 edition *supellex literaria* (LB, II, 402DE)—a phrase that signals a crucial change in Erasmus' thinking about the classical literary tradition. For in his earlier work, as we have seen, he figures this same tradition as *supellex Aegyptia*, despoiled Egyptian property.[23]

With this change, I am arguing, comes no small gain. Now imaginatively understood not as enemies but as joint-owners of a common inheritance, these same Christians, especially insofar as they read Erasmus' *Adages*, also become owners not only of a double inheritance but also of a richer notion of tradition itself. Alongside the scriptural figure from Exodus of the classical tradition as private property handed over through subterfuge or fraud to an enemy, Erasmus adds another figure—this one from the very classical literature he longs to reclaim and more particularly from Pythagorean coffers: common property shared freely among friends. It is finally in friendship, then, that Eras-

22. On the friendship between theology and philosophy see Adage IV. v. 1; LB, II, 1053F and Augustijn, 100.

23. The dedicatory letters to both the 1508 Aldine edition and the 1515 Froben edition refer to literary property as *supellex*. In the first case, Erasmus refers to the supply of Greek books (*Graecanorum librorum supellex*) that made his Aldine revisions possible (Ep. 211, Allen, I, 444; *CWE*, 2, 140); in the second, his lack of these same books (*Graecorum codicum supellex*) (Ep. 269, Allen, I, 523; *CWE*, 2, 243). In the earlier letter, moreover, he characterizes such literary forms as *sententiae* and *allegoriae poeticae* as *supellex* that adds richness (*ad locupletandam*) to one's style (Allen, I, 444; *CWE*, 2, 141).

mus professes not only to save but to reinvest so much of the classical literary tradition. His hopes in doing so, moreover, are those of any good Pythagorean. For with each investment, he will labor to leave the common store in no way depleted but, on the contrary, substantially enriched.

2

Friends and Lovers in the *Symposium:* Plato on Tradition

Fully in keeping with the literary agenda of the *Adages* to make available to Christian readers the common store of classical learning, Erasmus reconfigures the relation between the classical and Christian traditions from one between enemies to one between friends, not inappropriately replacing the patristic figure from Scripture of the Israelites despoiling the Egyptians with one from ancient philosophy as part of the newly reembraced classical past. As we have seen in the previous chapter, Erasmus' source for this replacement is first and foremost Pythagoras, father of both the saying that friends hold all things in common and the way of life it engenders; in second place, as we have also seen, Erasmus honors Plato, the ancient Italian philosopher's most influential disciple.

Taking seriously Erasmus' claims about the commonality found in Pythagorean, Platonic, and Christian philosophy, the next few chapters consider in more detail the Platonic and Pythagorean ideas that define the *Adages* as a literary project. Among these ideas are those epitomized in the opening adage: friendship and property. Also among them is the idea of tradition. As we have already seen, Erasmus distinguishes his own thinking about tradition, at least in the *Adages,* from that of such early Fathers of the Church as Origen, Tertullian, Jerome, and Augustine. As we will now see, Erasmus' understanding of tradition, like his understanding of friendship and property, looks back beyond his patristic sources to some of his favorite Platonic dialogues, including the *Republic,* the *Phaedrus,* the *Gorgias* and the *Symposium.* In these dialogues, and especially in the *Symposium,* as I hope to show in this chapter, Erasmus would find Plato's argument for the very philosophical tradition he claims to inherit. A thoughtful and thorough reader of Plato, as the *Adages* attests, Erasmus would also find Pythagoras at the center of Plato's brief.

Long before Erasmus' *Adages,* that is, Plato himself celebrates Pythagoras precisely for handing down to his followers a way of life. And it is this particular legacy, Plato claims, that sets Pythagoras apart from the more traditionally celebrated teacher of men (*Republic* 600AB):[1]

> are we told that, when Homer was alive, he was a leader in the education (*hēgemōn paideias*) of certain people who took pleasure in associating (*epi synousia*) with him in private and that he passed on (*paredosan*) a Homeric way of life to those who came after him, just as Pythagoras did? Pythagoras is particularly loved for this, and even today his followers are conspicuous for what they call the Pythagorean way of life.

Not the poet but the philosopher, Plato insists, educates men into living the most valuable lives (cf. 607B). And if the tradition preserves Homer's status as the poet of poets, it also hands down Pythagoras' status—familiar to Erasmus, as we have seen in the previous chapter—as not only the first philosopher but

1. Plato, *Republic,* trans. G. M. A. Grube (Indianapolis, 1992). And see Walter Burkert, *Lore and Science in Ancient Pythagoreanism,* trans. Edwin L. Minar, Jr. (Cambridge, Mass., 1972), esp. 83–96. I will discuss *paradosis* and education in chapter 4.

also the first to philosophize about the kinds of lives available for our choosing.

So one of Pythagoras' late antique biographies available to Erasmus leaves it on record (58):[2]

> Pythagoras is said to have been the first person to call himself a philosopher. It was not just a new word that he invented: he used it to explain a concern special to him. He said that people approach life like the crowds that gather at a festival. People come from all around, for different reasons: one is eager to sell his wares and make a profit, another to win fame by displaying his physical strength; and there is a third kind, the best sort of free men, who come to see places and fine craftsmanship and excellence in action and words, such as are generally on display at festivals. Just so, in life, people with all kinds of concerns assemble in one place. Some hanker after money and an easy life; some are in the clutches

2. *Iamblichi de vita pythagorica liber,* ed. L. Deubner (Leipzig, 1937); Iamblichus, *On the Pythagorean Life,* trans. Gillian Clark (Liverpool, 1989). On Pythagoras as the first philosopher, see also Isocrates, *Busiris,* 28–29; Cicero, *Tusc. Disp.,* V, 8–10; Diogenes Laertius, 8.8 and Augustine, *City of God,* 8.2.

On the identification of Pythagoras with the contemplative life of the philosopher, see *The Dialogues of Plato: The Symposium,* trans. and comm. R. E. Allen (New Haven, 1991), 85–86 and L. B. Carter, *The Quiet Athenian* (Oxford, 1986), 133–37, esp. 134: "The triple division of occupations—money-making, politics, philosophy—to which Pythagoras referred in the anecdote, must also, I think, be the work of Plato; in the *Republic* it forms the foundation of his whole analysis of contemporary society." On the Renaissance reception of this story, see S. K. Heninger, Jr., *Touches of Sweet Harmony: Pythagorean Cosmology and Renaissance Poetics* (San Marino, Calif., 1974), 29–30.

of desire for power and of frantic competition for fame; but the person of the greatest authority is the one who has chosen the study (*theōrian*) of that which is finest, and that one we call a philosopher.

Recording this admittedly self-promoting figure of the festival of life, the so-called *Vita Pythagorica* of the fourth-century Platonist Iamblichus lays out in detail the characteristics of the third of these three lives, that of the philosopher. And while Iamblichus attributes the figure to Pythagoras, he, like Erasmus after him, would also have encountered it unattributed in Plato's dialogues—in the *Republic*, for instance, where Socrates typifies individuals according to what their souls desire: profit for the *philokerdēs*, victory for the *philonikos* and wisdom for the *philosophos* (581BE). Alike in looking back to Pythagoras, these two competitions or *agones*—the one between the poet and the philosopher, the other between the three ways of life—predictably overlap. For any controversy over what we hold of value is likely to encourage argument over who is in charge of not only keeping the valued goods safe but also passing them on.

As we will see in more detail in chapter 4, the *Republic* is the Platonic dialogue most closely associated not only with these related *agones* but also with the proverbial wisdom that friends hold all things in common. It is not, however, the only dialogue well known to Erasmus to make this association. The *Symposium*—the source of the Erasmian adage "Sileni Alcibiadis" that introduced the previous chapter—weaves together these same two contests in order to explore erotic love as the motivating force behind tradition, especially the philosophical tradition.[3] Erasmus, then, begins by figuring the traditionary relation

---

3. On the three lives, see also *Phaedo* 68C, 82C and cf. *Nicomachean Ethics*, 1, 1095b17–22. And see L. B. Carter, *The Quiet Athenian*, esp.

as one between enemies only to reconfigure that relation, with Plato's help, as one between friends. Arguably the first to pose the problem of tradition, as we will now see, Plato figures the traditionary relation as one between lovers. But Plato's lovers, as Erasmus understood, also happen to be friends.

Although the *Symposium* is regularly and rightly identified as a dialogue about erotic love, the problem of tradition, posed in the language of friendship, fuels the rhetorical contest among the friends and lovers at Agathon's victory celebration. Before the contest begins, however, both the narrative and dramatic settings that introduce the dialogue also introduce the under-lying conflicts that set its course.[4] In the first place, Apollodorus' opening words draw a sharp distinction between himself and his unnamed interlocutor on the basis of their competing ways of life. Although Apollodorus has chosen the philosophical life in choosing to follow Socrates, his anonymous *hetairos* is a practical man—one who prefers action, even business, to contemplation (173C; cf. 172C–173A). And if Apollodorus' opening words signal the *agōn* between two ways of life broadly sketched, Socrates' opening words to Aristodemus alert us to that between the poet and the philosopher for the right to teach men how to live the lives they choose.

Playfully extending Agathon's dinner invitation to Aristode-mus at least implicitly on the proverbial grounds that friends hold all things in common, Socrates more explicitly adduces as

---

131–86. For the relation among these three dialogues, both thematic and chronological, see Paul Friedlaender, *Plato* (Princeton, 1969), III, 63–64, 120, 447–56.

4. On the importance of the "dramatic parts of the dialogue" see Allen, 3–5; Helen H. Bacon, "Socrates Crowned," *The Virginia Quarterly Review,* 35 (1959), 415–30 and Martha Nussbaum, "The Speech of Alci-biades: A Reading of Plato's Symposium," *Philosophy and Literature,* 3 (1979), 131–72, esp. 134–39.

proof two other proverbs. The first, recorded by Erasmus in the first *chilias*, concerns good men dining together (174B).[5] In contrast to Homer, who is here accused of outraging (*hubrisai*) the proverb, Socrates, as if following Erasmus' advice in the *Prolegomena* to the *Adages*, confesses merely to changing (*metaballein*) it to suit the occasion (174B; cf. LB, II, 1B, *CWE*, 31, 30). Socrates then invokes a second proverb, this one also recorded in the *Adages:* Diomedes' words in the *Iliad* affirming the need for comradeship in epic feats of daring (10. 224)—"As we proceed the two of us along the way." Here again, however, Socrates undermines the Homeric sentiment by allowing his companion Aristodemus to make his way to Agathon's all alone (174DE).[6]

Finding his place beside Agathon only after this proverbial sparring with Homer, Socrates replies to the poet's proposition to lie down beside him—so that, in Agathon's words (175D), "if I touch you, I may catch a bit of the wisdom that came to you under my neighbor's porch"—with words that resonate with a tension that goes well beyond the erotic joke. "How wonderful it would be," Socrates answers Agathon (175DE):

5. Athenaeus records the proverb as follows (*The Deipnosophists*, trans. Charles Burton Gulick, LCL [London, 1927],) I, 8A: "A brave man I, among brave men I have come to dine. For common are the goods of friends (*koina gar ta tōn philōn*)." See also *Adages*, I.x.35 (LB, II, 377E-378C; *CWE*, 32, 249-50), which cites the *Symposium*. And see R. G. Bury, *The Symposium of Plato* (Cambridge, 1909), 8-10.

6. On this Homeric quotation see also *Protagoras* 348D, discussed below, *Nicomachean Ethics*, 8.1, 1155a15 and *Adages*, III.i.51; *CWE*, 34, 200. And see Bury, 10.

On the *agōn* between poet and philosopher in this dialogue, see Bacon, 427-29 and Richard Patterson, "The Platonic Art of Comedy and Tragedy," *Philosophy and Literature*, 6 (1982), 78-93. Patterson also touches on the three ways of life (89). For a later statement of the rivalry see *Laws* 817AD.

For Plato's competition with Homer, see Longinus, 13.4.

if the foolish were filled with wisdom simply by touching the wise. If only wisdom were like water, which always flows from a full cup into an empty one when we connect them with a piece of yarn— well, then I would consider it the greatest prize to have the chance to lie down next to you. I would soon be overflowing with your wonderful wisdom.

As the conversation progresses, of course, the interlocutors will consider just how various substances flow from one human being to another, including the full range from semen to knowledge. Along the way they will assess the worth or value of the thing transmitted. At this particular moment, however, Socrates' serio-ludic reply deflates not only Agathon's sexual advance but, even more pointedly, the very grounds of their encounter. For the highest prize, Socrates implies, is surely not the one granted Agathon the day before yesterday at the dramatic festival. While Athenian culture at large may so honor its tragic performances and the poets who produce them, and while even the poets themselves, coveting these honors, may enjoy the pleasures of *philotimia*, Socrates, for one, places his value elsewhere.[7]

Sharply differentiating the philosopher from the poet, Socrates' reply also enables Plato to call into question the traditional instruments of tradition. Unlike the water in the homespun image above that passes substantially unaltered between two cups, knowledge, or at least information, changes in substance as it passes from speaker to listener. Resembling the poet's internal tales, Apollodorus' report to Aristodemus, on the teller's own account, inevitably fails to render the conversation exactly, word for word, but rather, as Apollodorus says, "what he remembered

7. See *Republic* 568AC and Friedlaender, 77.

best, and what I consider the most important points" (178A)—
in the Greek *axiomnēmoneuton,* what is worth remembering.[8]

Herein lies the problem with traditional learning: one passes
on what one remembers and one remembers what one honors
or considers valuable, dooming the rest to devaluation and even
oblivion. Despite Apollodorus' special preparedness for the task
—he repeats that he is *ouk ameletētos* (172A, 173C)—he nevertheless passes on to his listener, as readers regularly note, a round
of speeches far removed from what was actually said: not an
exact likeness but, to anticipate Diotima's language of begetting, a reproduction. Passed on from Aristodemus to Apollodorus and from Apollodorus to his companion and to us, the
speeches themselves work together to set before us tradition
itself as the problematic.

Arguing that love is worthy of honor because it promotes love
of honor or *philotimia* (179A, 179E–180A), Phaedrus seems to
formulate his encomium in traditional terms. Citing the works
of the past, especially the poets, including Homer, Hesiod and
Euripides, he locates the battlefield as the principal arena for
excellent or virtuous action. In actuality, however, Phaedrus
manipulates his traditional sources and material the better to accommodate his argument. For it is surely not the case, as Phaedrus claims, that "[w]hen Homer says a god 'breathes might'
into some of the heroes, this is really Love's gift to every lover"
(179B). According to Phaedrus' interpretation, however, the
gods honor Alcestis and Achilles specifically for their courage
in love (179D).

Indeed, while Phaedrus seems to be arguing from tradition
and traditional values, he is actually reconceiving that tradition

8. According to LSJ there is no instance of this word before Plato and
Xenophon. See also *Republic* 551A and Bury, 21.

in terms of his own culture, recasting the figures of the past into the contemporary relation of *erastēs* or lover and *erōmenos* or *paidika*, the beloved. So, on Phaedrus' far-fetched account, Achilles wins greater honor than Alcestis for the excellence motivated by love because less is expected from the beloved— in Phaedrus' reading of the *Iliad* Achilles' relation to Patroklos—than from the lover—his reading of Alcestis' relation to her husband Admetus (179B ff.). While Phaedrus' appropriation of tradition in the form of these traditional stories is clumsily handled, Plato's point is not. As Apollodorus has already inadvertently signaled, there is no neutral handling of tradition, and the reception of the past, as Phaedrus unintentionally proves, is always, in the terms of one contemporary theorist of tradition, a fusing of horizons.[9]

By focusing on the relationship of lover to beloved, Phaedrus' speech alerts us to the power of tradition itself for relocating cultural value. In second position, Pausanias' speech as recounted by Apollodorus advances Plato's agenda by redefining the relationship between lover and beloved as itself an instrument of tradition. Whereas Phaedrus' Love renders the lover *philonikos*— in love with victory—Pausanias' Love fosters rather *philia* and *koinōnia*, friendship and community, the elements of Erasmus' opening proverb (182C). Indeed, the lover who offers his beloved either political power or wealth—the desired goals of two of the three lives featured in both the *Republic* and the Iamblichan *Vita Pythagorica*—deserves shame rather than honor. Only the lover motivated to embrace the objective of the third way of life, namely wisdom, merits approval (184B). As Pausanias defines it, in other words, the role of the lover is actively to hand

9. For the role of this fusing of horizons in the development of tradition see Hans-Georg Gadamer, *Truth and Method*, esp. 302–307.

down knowledge to the beloved, to educate him, while the role of the beloved is passively to receive knowledge, to be educated (184CE):

> If someone decides to put himself at another's disposal because he thinks that this will make him better in wisdom or in any other part of virtue, we approve of his voluntary subjection . . . and when the lover *is* able to help the young man become wiser and better, and the young man *is* eager to be taught and improved by his lover—then, and only then, when these two principles coincide absolutely, is it ever honorable for a young man to accept a lover.

The traditionary value—as distinguished from the traditional value—of love (here specifically male homosexual love) renders it worthwhile according to Pausanias, an honored custom that sets Athenian culture apart. And just as the Athenians honor other forms of contest that promote both excellence and friendship, such as philosophical discussion and sports, so they honor the male homoerotic relationship, which fosters these same values.[10]

If Phaedrus rewrites the tradition to honor love, Pausanias honors, in particular, love's traditionary power—its spur to the most excellent life. Following them, Eryximachus extends the boundaries of both love and tradition to include natural philosophy, of which medicine, his own profession, is a part. Here as elsewhere in the dialogues, moreover, Plato has Socrates set

---

10. That Plato would not acquiesce in Pausanias' argument and does not expect the reader to is implied not least in the speaker's positive use of such characteristically pejorative terms in a Platonic context as *poikilos* (182B; cf. 218C) and *megala phronēmata* (182C; cf. 190B). See Bury, xxvi–xxvii, 36 and 154.

himself apart from these natural philosophers. He is not, as he claims in the *Apology* for example, to be confused with Anaxagoras (26D), whose teachings are readily available in the marketplace.[11] Indeed, moral philosophy begins its long career with Plato antagonistic to—in competition with—the natural philosophy that Eryximachus expounds. Even though Eryximachus claims to build on Pausanias' speech and take as his theme the higher and lower forms of love, the profitable resolution of conflict, the harmony of opposites, and integration or wholeness (all recurring motifs throughout the dialogue[12]), he claims these powers not only for love but for the first teacher of all physicians, Asclepius, and thus ultimately for himself (186DE):

> A good practitioner knows how to affect the body and to transform (*metaballein*) its desires; he can implant the proper species of Love when it is absent and eliminate the other sort whenever it occurs. The physician's task is to effect a reconciliation and establish mutual love (*phila*) between the most basic bodily elements. . . . In fact, our ancestor Asclepius first established medicine as a profession when he learned how to produce concord and love between such opposites—that is what those poet fellows say, and—this time—I concur with them.

Conceding authority here to the poets, the traditional preservers of tradition, presumably because in this instance they uphold his own authority, Eryximachus makes extravagant claims for natural philosophy: it promotes harmony in both the body and the body politic; it fosters friendship or *philia* between gods and men

---

11. See Carter, *The Quiet Athenian*, 141–54.

12. On the Pythagorean origin of these elements see Bury, 50–51 and 58 and William S. Cobb, *Plato's Erotic Dialogues* (Albany, 1993), 66–67.

(cf. 188D); and it has the power to transform or change (*meta-ballein*) our desires—to uproot one desire and replace it with another.

It is in the context of this last and most extraordinary claim, moreover, that we should understand Eryximachus' willingness to take Aristophanes' place during the poet's attack of hiccups. By doing so, Eryximachus upsets at least temporarily the customary or traditional order of speakers from left to right (185DE), thus enabling his own profession to speak in place of the poets, whom Aristophanes represents. With this first of four interruptions, in other words, Plato sets the stakes with unmistakable clarity; the *agōn* here is for the very right to control human desire, to determine what we should love and hold worthy of value.

So at least Aristophanes has understood the stakes. For he begins by reaffirming the traditionary power of poetry (189D): "I shall, therefore, try to explain [Love's] power to you; and you, please pass my teaching on to everyone else." He then proceeds, in true poetic fashion, to recount a most compelling originary myth, taking as his theme not only our first bodily forms but also our first desires. Granted integration by the gods—here as often in Plato figured as circularity—human beings desired to overcome these same gods. Like Homer's stories and like Plato's own dialogue, Aristophanes' tale is one of contest, of the *agōn*. The punishment for competing with the gods—the cost, that is, of misplaced desire, as Aristophanes describes it—is physical disintegration and the attendant transformation of desire. Whereas in our integrated state we desired power, in our disintegrated state, we desire integration. And sex, according to this myth, is a second-order desire, the physical manifestation of a psychological need for reintegration (191D). Love, on Aristophanes' account, is our name for the desire to be whole or complete (192E).

So consuming, in fact, is this need for reintegration that

Aristophanes' lovers, resembling the victims of Homer's Sirens, neglect all other bodily needs, dying in an endless embrace (191AB). Finally, in an effort to avoid the annihilation of the race, Zeus transforms their means of reproduction from that of the cicadas to sexual intercourse, in this way allowing, even if only temporarily, the reunification of divided halves.[13] Rewriting Homer's erotic tale of Aphrodite and Ares sung by Demodokos (*Odyssey*, 8.266–366), Aristophanes further imagines an Hephaistos willing and able to use his skill in binding not for the purposes of thwarting adulterous lovers but for reuniting devoted lovers together forever. For holding all things in common (*koinēi*), including life and death, is what such lovers really desire (192DE).[14]

In the hands of the poet as teacher of men, however, the erotic tale serves not only an idealizing but also a cautionary function. In keeping with our bodily transformations, that is, Zeus exhorts us to contemplate (*theasthai*) our condition (190E); for it

13. Both the *Symposium* (191BC; cf. 216A) and the *Phaedrus* (230C, 258E–259D) associate the Sirens with the cicadas and both with the attraction of philosophical discourse. In the *Symposium,* human beings in their integrated state resembled cicadas in not experiencing desire for one another but rather reproducing separately in the ground. It is only in their disintegrated state that they become more fully human by acquiring sexuality both for reproductive and therapeutic purposes. In the *Phaedrus,* on the contrary, the evolution is reversed. There human beings become cicadas as a consolation for their fatal addiction to the pleasures of song. Both myths feature a desire so strong that it overwhelms physical survival, emphasizing in the human condition ineradicable needs beyond mere survival whose temporary satisfaction is experienced as pleasure. In both cases, Plato's term for the impulse to fulfill these needs, the drive towards pleasure, is *erōs.*

For Plato's evolving attitudes toward pleasure see Friedlaender, 120. See also Bury, 61–62.

14. In the *Politics* (2.1, 1262b10–11), Aristotle characterizes the relation between Aristophanes' lovers as excessive friendship.

is only through contemplation—in this case on the scar as reminder of our misdeeds—that we become more orderly (*kosmōteroi*).[15] Otherwise, Aristophanes cautions, we may be halved again. "We should encourage all men," he warns, "to treat the gods with all due reverence, so that we may escape this fate and find wholeness instead" (193B). By passing on these stories of misplaced desire, then, the poets impel us to lead better—more contemplative—lives.

In Aristophanes' speech, in other words, it is the office of the poet and not of the natural philosopher to transform our desires. And this contest for control of human desire, for the privilege of determining what we value and how we live, continues not only in the next two speeches, as we will see momentarily, but also in the second interruption of the established order—Socrates' attempt to preempt Agathon's discourse by substituting his own discursive method (194CD).

While it resembles the earlier bout of hiccups in disguising an attempt to relocate authority, Socrates' interruption at 194CD advances Plato's agenda even further by drawing our attention more specifically to the question of method, to the instrument or procedure for imparting knowledge. For though a tragedian, Agathon, here acclaimed a student of Gorgias, represents not just the poetic but also the sophistic tradition. And we do well once again to recall not only the historical antagonism between philosophy and sophistic but also Socrates' repeated attempts throughout the dialogues to distinguish himself from this group of professionals.[16]

15. Cf. 194AB, 210D and see Bury, 127. On the Pythagorean origins of both contemplation or *theōria* and order or *kosmos*, see below.

16. Plato's attack on the sophists and their educational program constitutes an offensive that spans the entire range of his dialogues. See the discussion of the *Protagoras* below.

In view of the focus of Socrates' aborted interruption and Agathon's affiliation, the latter's speech begins not surprisingly with a statement of method (194E–195A) and then continues somewhat incoherently to fulfill its own expectations, praising both the qualities and the benefits of Love. Contesting Phaedrus' more traditional view of an ancient *Erōs*, Agathon's Love is young and physically attractive. Contesting Aristophanes' more profound vision of integration, Agathon's Love overpowers even Ares, motivating the adulterous desire that cuckolds the very Hephaistos who offered to bind devoted lovers together in the previous speech (196D). Indeed, it is wholly fitting that Agathon's sophistic oratory concentrate on Love's outward appearance, his physical beauty and strength; and no less fitting is Agathon's characterization of Love's intellectual virtues, his wisdom or *sophia*.

Echoing in fact Agathon's earlier invitation to Socrates to join him on the couch so that some of his guest's newly acquired wisdom might rub off, Love's wisdom is here described by Agathon as transmitted simply by touching (196DE):

> In the first place — to honor *our* profession as Eryximachus did his — the god is so skilled a poet that he can make others into poets: once Love touches him, *anyone* becomes a poet ". . . however uncultured he had been before."

Agathon's claim here for Love's easy transmission of knowledge to *anyone* and *everyone* targets the same program of sophistic education criticized, as we will see in the next chapter, in the *Protagoras*. According to Plato, the sophists assured wisdom, or at least *technē*, skill, to anyone who could afford the tuition. In this sense precisely, the sophists were masters of technique. And Agathon's Love is just such a master. "And as for artisans and professionals," Agathon boasts (197A), " — don't we know that whoever has this god for a teacher ends up in the light of fame, while a man untouched by Love ends in obscurity." Like the sophist himself, Love, the professional teacher of professional technicians, endows his pupils with the skills and techniques necessary to success and fame. Love, in other words, passes on to them the knowledge—or at least the "know-how"—necessary to positions of honor, not unlike that of Agathon himself at the dramatic festival.

At last, it is Socrates' turn. He introduces his contribution to the contest of speeches by returning to the question of method, a question rendered even more urgent by Agathon's well-received display. For Socrates must now distinguish himself not only from the poets and the natural philosophers but also from the sophists, whose methods were most easily confused with his own. In addition to boldly rejecting sophistic method, therefore, Socrates also takes the opportunity to point up its inadequacy. Characteristic of sophistic discourse, which, according to Plato, is lacking in both form and matter, Agathon's speech has failed to distinguish between the method of inquiry and its object. Through question and answer—Socrates' own untraditional method—he establishes with Agathon that desire is love or desire of an object. Armed with this agreement, Socrates shifts the aim of the discussion from defining Love as what we honor—to praise love, after all, is to honor it—to defining rather what we love—the *object* of desire or love and not desire or love itself.

With this newly formulated question in mind, Socrates invokes his own teacher, Diotima, whose name signifies ambiguously "god-honoring" and "god-honored" and who, in Socrates' words, resembles the perfect sophist (208C; cf. 203E). With this invocation of his teacher, he also returns us to the central problematic of tradition, only here the instrument of tradition is glaringly untraditional: instead of the male/male relationship upheld earlier as both traditional and traditionary, Socrates introduces a male/female relationship, in which even more glaringly the female is the older, active agent of knowledge and the male the younger, passive recipient, although Plato certainly makes clear that the lines of transmission are not necessarily so gendered.[17] For Socrates' questioning of Agathon hands down, he notes, Diotima's earlier questioning of him, even though, as he admits recalling Apollodorus' earlier disclaimer, he doesn't remember the exact words of their exchange (201DE).

In keeping with the untraditional origins of this tradition, moreover, Diotima sometimes uses traditional forms of knowledge, such as the myths of the poets, but fills them, as did Aristophanes, with strikingly untraditional material. Recalling both Phaedrus' questionable claim at the opening of this dialogue that we lack speeches in praise of love (177CD)[18] and Socrates' examination of Agathon moments earlier, Diotima recounts that *Erōs* was begotten by *Poros* and *Penia*—Resourcefulness and Poverty—precisely to get *Penia*, his mother, what she lacks. Desire or love, as Socrates has already argued, signifies not an object but the lack of one.

Decidedly not the more casual touching of the sophist, then, Diotima's loving is rather a begetting, a bringing forth into being (as *Poros* does in *Penia*) that characterizes a multiplicity of human experiences. Despite the popular restriction of *erōs*, like *poiēsis* or poetry, to only one kind of experience, there are many different kinds of love: some people love money, some love athletic competitions, and some love philosophy (205D). Not only rehearsing the three lives enumerated by Pythagoras but also granting the highest status to the third or philosophical life,

17. Phaedrus' reading of the story of Alcestis and Admetus (179BC) prepares us for this untraditional relation.

18. See Bury, 19.

Diotima at the same time insists that even the offspring of this best kind of life, namely knowledge, comes to be and passes away, no less than a child, which is also an object of love, if a lesser one in the context of this dialogue.

The sustaining of knowledge, like that of physical life, in other words, depends on renewal over time. Remarking on the strangeness of this claim, Diotima insists nevertheless on its truth (208A):

> And what is still far stranger than that is that not only does one branch of knowledge come to be in us while another passes away and that we are never the same even in respect of our knowledge, but that each single piece of knowledge has the same fate. For what we call studying (*meletan*) exists because knowledge is leaving us, because forgetting is the departure of knowledge, while studying (*meletē*) puts back a fresh memory in place of what went away, thereby preserving a piece of knowledge, so that it seems to be the same. And in that way everything mortal is preserved, not, like the divine, by always being the same in every way, but because what is departing and aging leaves behind something new, something such as it had been.

Requiring both preservation and transmission, in other words, human knowledge contrasts with divine in never being the same, but always, like the human generations, at once similar to and different from its bearers and forebears. Apollodorus' repeated assurance that he has recently reviewed the tale he is about to tell —that he is not *ameletētos*—has already sensitized us to this process of transmission. So has Phaedrus' clumsy use of tradition in the opening speech of the contest. Recalling Apollodorus' words with her own insistence on the need for *meletē*, Diotima similarly returns to Phaedrus' earlier misunderstanding—or perhaps partial understanding—of the past, especially the myths of Alcestis and Achilles. For neither would have died for those they loved if the ultimate object of their love had not been immortality (208D). Indeed, for humankind, more generally, this is what it means to love what we lack. And whereas some lovers pursue immortality through physical offspring, others strive to leave behind the products of intellectual intercourse.

Echoing both Pausanias' and Aristophanes' speeches, Diotima characterizes this better brand of lover as one who begins by sharing conversation with his beloved in an effort to educate him. Her brand of love combines, moreover, the two features of the opening adage: friendship and commonality—*philia* and *koinōnia* (209C):

> Together (*koinēi*) with him he nurtures the offspring produced, so that such men have much more to share (*koinōnian*) with each other and a stronger friendship (*philian*) than that which comes from rearing children, since they share (*kekoinōnēkotes*) in the rearing of children who are more beautiful and more immortal.

Like the friends of the Pythagorean proverb in sharing the objectives of the philosophical life, Diotima's lovers also recall Aristophanes' in neglecting their bodily needs. But while Aristophanes' lovers would waste away beholding a beloved held in a physical embrace, Diotima's lose themselves beholding something beyond any physical grasp. And whereas the Aristophanic lovers are enjoined to contemplate the cause of their bodily transformation to fragmented pieces of a whole, Diotima's lovers are motivated instead to gaze directly upon (*theasthai*) wholeness and immutability (211DE). For this is the life, Diotima concludes, of those befriended by the gods (*theophiles*) (212AB; cf. 193B).[19]

Skillfully deployed to reinforce the *agōn* between poet and philosopher, Socrates' appropriation through Diotima of elements of Aristophanes' speech are not lost on the poet himself, whose protest is silenced only by Alcibiades' unannounced entrance (212C). The third of four interruptions, Alcibiades has come to honor Agathon for his victory in the dramatic contest. And if unexpected, his arrival is surely not fortuitous; for it allows Plato to balance the doctrine of the teacher with the testimony of the student, thus completing the trajectory that defines traditional learning.

Plato even has Alcibiades draw the reader's attention to the force of this relation, reminding his listeners both that Olympus owes all his tunes to his music teacher, Marsyas (215C), and that even the duller students of Socrates, a latter-day Marsyas, stun their audiences when they repeat the lessons of their master (215D). So powerful are these lessons especially as Socrates teaches them that Alcibiades himself fears the same fate as Homer's Sirens and Aristophanes' lovers; lacking Odysseus' courage, he stops his ears, "so that I won't grow old just sitting there beside him" (216A). Just the sight of Socrates, as we witness for ourselves, is enough to distract Alcibiades from his stated project of crowning Agathon.

This distraction—Alcibiades' turning from Agathon to Socrates—does more, however, than simply reopen the *agōn* between poet and philosopher drowned out moments earlier by all the commotion. It also advances the other, related competition

19. For the philosopher as *philotheamonos*, see *Republic* 475E and as *theophilēs* see *Republic* 612E and *Protagoras* 345C. On *theasthai*, see Cobb, 80.

that has so far structured this dialogue. In the final round of the contest, the debate over who should teach us how to live takes account once more of the kind of life it should be. And Plato's masterful characterization of Alcibiades sets in high relief that the *agōn* between competing ways of life ultimately takes as its battleground the individual human soul. For Alcibiades, unlike the nameless *hetairos* who questions Apollodorus, is torn between the fatal attractions of political life, figured most persuasively in the oratory of Pericles (215E, 221C), and the irresistible tug of the philosophical life, whose even more seductive spokesman is Socrates (215E–216B):[20]

> I have heard Pericles and many other great orators, and I have admired their speeches. But nothing like this has ever happened to me . . . my very own soul started protesting that my life — *my* life — was no better than the most miserable slave's. . . . He always traps me, you see, and he makes me admit that my political career is a waste of time, while all that matters is just what I most neglect: my personal shortcomings, which cry out for the closest attention. . . . Yes, he makes me feel ashamed: I know perfectly well that I can't prove he's wrong when he tells me what I should do; yet, the moment I leave his side,

20. Clearly Plato himself has learned a great deal from Thucydides' Pericles. Like Pausanias and even Diotima, the idealized statesman, faced with the task of praising those who died in the war's first year, characterizes them as lovers and reckons their worth according to the worth of their beloved city. In light of this strategy, he spends nearly his entire speech praising Athens and exhorts his listeners to imitate those who have died in falling in love with her (II, 42–43).

On the worst kind of discord as internal, psychological discord, see *Gorgias* 482C.

I go back to my old ways: I cave in to my desire to please the crowd.

Characterized as locked in combat with himself over whether to choose the life of *philotimia* or *philosophia,* Alcibiades in turn characterizes Socrates as free from such internal conflict. In the ultimate battle — that for self-mastery — the philosopher puts up the best fight.

Only the philosopher, as Alcibiades has witnessed firsthand, drinks without getting drunk, feasts without giving way to appetite, enjoys physical intimacy without becoming sexually aroused, and fights valiantly without coveting the political rewards that accompany such heroism (218C–219D, 220A–221C). More than the others, the philosopher so orders experience that the lesser pleasures are subordinated to the greater. Hardly an "ascetic" in Alcibiades' portrait, Socrates feels as fully as anyone the press of desire.[21] More to the point, he not only desires the objects of greatest value but spends his time — nearly all his time — laboring to transform the desires of others, begetting in them love for these same objects.

In the contest for control of human desire, however, the philosopher competes not only with Aristophanes' poet but also with Eryximachus' doctor and Agathon's sophist. They too claim the right to teach us how to live. Admittedly with Plato's help, Socrates defeats their claims; but he does so less by his tolerance for drink than by his skill in integrating in a way worthy of the philosopher's soul the methods and insights of his competitors. As both practiced and preached in the *Symposium,* philosophical discourse prevails because it is as dramatic as tragedy, as persuasive as sophistic oratory and as therapeutic as medicine.

21. I will return below to the important issue of asceticism. For the subordination of lesser to greater pleasures see *Republic* 561AC.

Skillful in its use of story and argument, it promises to effect in at least some if not in all of its students a recognition of ignorance and error, a reversal of previous wrong actions and greater psychic health. By the time the fourth and final interruption—the band of drunken revelers—carries Alcibiades off not only to further internal conflict but also to political disaster, the other contest, the one for the right both to determine cultural value and to beget that value in others, has been decided. Its offspring, embraced by Erasmus centuries later, is the Western philosophical tradition.[22]

22. In *The Structure and Date of Book 10 of Plato's "Republic"* (Heidelberg, 1972), Gerald Else makes this point (60): "Plato's foundation of the Akademy had been a manifestation of faith in the sole right of Philosophy to guide the lives of men. In his eyes, one of the first corollaries of that faith was that Poetry must abdicate its ancient calling to do the same. The 'difference' between Poetry and Philosophy was total and ineluctable: every man must choose. And—perhaps after some initial hesitation and confusion—many promising young men from all over the Greek world had indeed chosen Philosophy. We may take as their type and example the young Aristotle, who came to the Akademy in 367 at the age of 17 and never left it until after Plato's death."

3

Plato on Proverbial Wisdom and the Philosophical Life

With the *Symposium*, as we have seen in the previous chapter, Plato both gives the question of traditionality philosophical attention and makes his case for the philosophical tradition as the best means of education. Grounded in friendship or *philia*, this tradition moreover owes its genesis to its adversarial relation with poetry and sophistry. Prevailing over poet and sophist, Plato's philosopher, as characterized in this dialogue, passes on to his students not just an education but an educated way of life. The value of this way of life, the philosopher's role in passing it on and its compatibility with *philosophia Christi* echo throughout the *Adages*. The "Sileni Alcibiadis"—to take not only the most famous example but one that explicitly amplifies a bit of the *Symposium*—chastises princes and even more so priests for choosing the wrong kind of life and thereby proving themselves lovers of wealth and power rather than wisdom and virtue. For their correction, as we have already seen in chapter 1, this adage adduces not only Christ but also the Socrates of the *Symposium* as archetypal sileni and just such lovers of wisdom.

In the 1508 *Prolegomena* to the *Adages,* as we have also seen in chapter 1, Erasmus argues for the closest possible alignment between philosophy and proverbial statement. There he singles out Plato as not only the greatest philosopher but one without peer in the use of proverbs. Plato is, in Erasmus' words, *paroimiōdesteros*—the master of proverbs (LB, II, 5C). Indeed, Plato's dialogues themselves are understood by Erasmus to amplify a more remote ancient wisdom preserved in this most compressed literary form. While citing the *Gorgias* and the *Republic* as examples of such philosophical amplification of proverbial wisdom, Erasmus portrays throughout the *Adages* a Plato who fully appreciates the proverb as an instrument of philosophy.[1]

Erasmus' portrait of Plato finds particular confirmation in the *Protagoras,* another dialogue cited throughout the *Adages.* Here Plato has Socrates reflect his appreciation for proverbs in his own argument against the eponymous sophist; for Socrates claims not only that the Spartans were the most advanced philosophically but that they philosophized by means of sayings at once brief and memorable — *brachea* and *axiomnēmoneuta* (342D–343C). By way of illustration, Socrates adduces two of the best-known adages included side by side in Erasmus' collection: "Know thyself" and "Nothing overmuch" (I.vi.95 and I.vi.96; LB, II, 258D–259E; *CWE*, 32, 62–64).[2]

Alike in drawing attention to things *axiomnēmoneuta,* the *Protagoras* and *Symposium* share in turn the problematic of tradition that this unusual term signals and that Erasmus inherits as part of his own tradition. Indeed, this shared focus forms part of a constellation of commonalities linking these two dialogues and even encouraging us to read them together. So the *hetairos* who listens to Socrates' account of his recent conversation with Protagoras begins his own conversation with Socra-

1. According to M. M. Phillips, only Aristophanes, Cicero, Homer, Horace, Plautus, and Plutarch, including pseudo-Plutarch, are cited more than Plato (393–403).

2. As discussed by Erasmus, both adages are attributed by somebody or other to Pythagoras.

On the confusion between Pythagoras and Protagoras see Charles Trinkaus, "Protagoras in the Renaissance: An Exploration," *Philosophy and Humanism: Renaissance Essays in Honor of Paul Oskar Kristeller,* ed. Edward P. Mahoney (Leiden, 1976), 190–213.

tes by inquiring about his affair with Alcibiades. With the exception of Aristophanes, in fact, all of the principal speakers at Agathon's drinking party also play some role on this occasion (315C–316A). Agathon's particular status as the poet-sophist in the *Symposium*, moreover, pinpoints the very aspect of tradition that in the *Protagoras* demands our full attention.

As we have seen, the *Symposium* dramatizes not only the *agōn* between competing ways of life, but also that between the professionals who would teach us how to live this best kind of life. The *Protagoras*, in turn, targets both the sophistic program of education—in contrast to the philosophical—that claims to prepare us for the best life and the foundational role of poetry in this program. For in the distant past, according to Protagoras, sophists such as Homer, Hesiod, and Simonides clothed their wisdom in verse (316D). Accordingly, Protagoras insists that "the greatest part of a man's education is to be skilled in the matter of verses; that is, to be able to apprehend, in the utterances of the poets, what has been rightly and wrongly composed" (338E–339A; cf. 325E–326A).[3] And for this same reason he challenges Socrates to a contest of literary exegesis.[4]

Socrates, in contrast, identifies the earliest wisdom literature with the philosophers, and especially with those who practiced the *brachylogia* most characteristic of the proverb (cf. *Gorgias* 449BC). Although willing to take up Protagoras' challenge—if only to consider the insight that Plato will explore more fully in the *Symposium* that each profession finds its own presuppositions

3. *Protagoras*, trans. W. R. M. Lamb, LCL (Cambridge, Mass., 1924; rpt. 1977).

4. See my *Hermeneutics and the Rhetorical Tradition*, 21–23.

One crucial distinction between philosophical and sophistic training is that the sophist, like the poet, sometimes praises tyranny, the philosopher never (346BC).

in its literary interpretations [5] — Socrates nevertheless compares the exercise of literary exegesis, the cornerstone of Protagorean pedagogy, to the wrong kind of symposium (347CE):

> For it seems to me that arguing about poetry is comparable to the wine-parties of common marketfolk. These people, owing to their inability to carry on a familiar conversation over their wine by means of their own voices and discussions — such is their lack of education — put a premium on flute girls by hiring the extraneous voice of the flute at a high price, and carry on their intercourse by means of its utterance. But where the party consists of thorough gentlemen who have had a proper education, you will see neither flute-girls nor dancing-girls nor harp-girls. ... And so a gathering like this of ours, when it includes such men as most of us claim to be, requires no extraneous voices, not even of the poets, whom one cannot question on the sense of what they say; when they are adduced in discussion we are generally told by some that the poet thought so and so, and by others, something different, and they go on arguing about a matter which they are powerless to determine.

Addressing issues central to the *Symposium* as well as the *Gorgias* and the *Phaedrus,* the *Protagoras* sets in opposition two competing educational programs, each advertising itself as preparation for the best kind of life and each passed on from generation to generation by a specially trained teacher.[6] In the Protagorean

5. See, for instance, 345DE, where Socrates asserts that both sophists and poets, including Simonides, presuppose that no one errs willingly.

6. There is in the *Protagoras,* most likely the earliest of the dialogues

program, that teacher is the sophist; in the Socratic, he is the philosopher. Here as in the *Symposium,* moreover, this competition between sophistic and philosophical training or education is simultaneously a competition for control over human desire, over what we should love and hold worthy of value. Accordingly, it is up to the teacher to transform our desires, to turn them toward the most worthwhile objects (cf. 318B and 348E–349D).

In the *Protagoras* as in the *Symposium,* in other words, Socrates questions both the traditionary value of poetry and the traditional role of the poet—and following him, the sophist—as the teacher of men. And in the *Protagoras,* as in the *Symposium,* Socrates freely uses the weapons of the poets in raising these questions. So the same proverbial line of Diomedes from the *Iliad* (10.224) that encouraged Aristodemus in the *Symposium* to join Agathon's party (174DE) serves here to chide the faltering Protagoras into persevering in his conversation with Socrates. In both cases, not incidentally, the philosopher invokes this proverb—"When two go together, one observes before the other"—to advocate communal life.[7] For however they may disagree

---

I am considering here, a third program of education that resembles the Pythagorean as it is more fully developed in the *Gorgias* and the *Republic* and that is compared very much in passing in this dialogue with the Protagorean. Of its teachers Protagoras says (318DE), "The generality of them maltreat the young; for when they have escaped from the arts they bring them back against their will and force them into arts, teaching them arithmetic and astronomy and geometry and music (and here he glanced at Hippias); whereas, if he applies to me, he will learn precisely and solely that for which he has come. That learning consists of good judgment in his own affairs, showing how best to order his own home; and in the affairs of his city, showing how he may have most influence on public affairs both in speech and in action."

7. On this proverb, including Erasmus' discussion of it in the *Adages,* see chap. 2, above. On the special ability of the adage to accommodate changing contexts, see Erasmus, *Prolegomena,* LB, II, 7B-8B, *CWE,* 31,

about the means and ends of the best life, that life—poet, sophist, and philosopher would agree—is communal: a *koinōnia* And disagreement (*amphisbētein*) itself, as Prodicus distinguishes it from the wrangling (*erizein*) of enemies, belongs to friendship as the basis of community (337AB). So, Socrates reflects aloud, it is not just words and deeds but even thinking that benefits from such *koinōnia* (348CD). On this issue of community, Homer's words spoken by Diomedes do indeed convey some proverbial wisdom.

Like the *Protagoras* and the *Symposium,* the *Gorgias* too takes as its task investigating the best—most valuable—way of life. As we have seen in the previous chapter, tradition attributes the earliest impulse to make such an inquiry to Pythagoras, the first philosopher. Whereas the *Symposium,* as we have also seen, outlines all three choices supposedly set out by the Italian philosopher, the *Gorgias,* explicitly invoking his authority, concentrates attention on the opposition between two of the three lives: the political and the philosophical. Choosing between them, Socrates insists, is the common focus of his conversation with all three interlocutors in this dialogue (500C):[8]

> For you see that our debate is upon a question which
> has the highest conceivable claims to the serious
> interest even of a person who has but little intelli
> gence—namely, what course of life is best; whether
> it should be that to which you invite me, with all
> those manly pursuits of speaking in Assembly and

15–17 and Aristotle, *Rhetoric,* 1.15, 1376a1, cited by Erasmus, and my "'Between Friends All is Common': The Erasmian Adage and Tradition," 409.

8. Plato, *Gorgias,* trans. W. R. M. Lamb, LCL (Cambridge, Mass., 1925; rpt. 1983).

practicing rhetoric (*rhētorikēn askounta*) and going in for politics after the fashion of you modern politicians, or this life of philosophy; and what makes the difference between the two.

Whereas Callicles, according to Socrates, resembles Alcibiades in being in love with the admiration of the people and the power that their esteem confers, Socrates, on his own account, loves Alcibiades and, even more so, philosophy (481D; cf. 513C). And whereas Callicles must continually change to suit his ever-shifting beloved, the people (481E), Socrates not only need not shift about in serving his beloved but also, recalling the office of the philosopher in the *Symposium,* must on the contrary labor to reorient others, including Alcibiades, to desiring objects at once more stable and more worthy of love (493CD). It is in the starkest contrast to Socrates, then, that Callicles considers philosophy worthwhile only for the young and only then as a preparation for political life (485C–486D).[9]

The last of three conversations structuring the *Gorgias,* the debate between Socrates and Callicles does most to advance the *agōn* between the two competing ways of life. As the last and most formidable of Socrates' interlocutors, moreover, Callicles also delivers in the opening words of the dialogue the very first blow of the competition. Not incidentally, his weapon in this brief skirmish is a proverb. Managing to duck Callicles' assault with a deadly saying—that he has conveniently arrived, like the coward of the adage, too late for the battle—Socrates disarms his opponent by substituting another, less provocative

9. Whereas in the philosophical tradition, as we see in the *Republic,* the liberal arts, including rhetoric, serve as propaedeutic for philosophy, in the rhetorical tradition, philosophy serves as a propaedeutic for political life.

adage: not too late for the fight, Socrates spars, but for the feast (447A).[10] Introducing both the agonistic and culinary analogies that will pervade the conversation, Plato also has Socrates introduce more particularly the context for his later argument with Callicles. For fighting differs from feasting in that the former activity brings enemies together, the latter, friends. Here as in the *Symposium*, that is, friendship or *philia* provides a framework for examining not only the rhetorical art but the political life it claims to foster. Without explicitly invoking the Pythagorean proverb about *philia* and *koinōnia*, as we shall see, Plato grounds his refutation of the Calliclean way of life in an examination of these and other unmistakably Pythagorean principles.

It is imperative, moreover, that Socrates refute Callicles. For the "natural justice" that Callicles promotes authorizes each individual to claim for himself as much as he can hope to retain by force (483E–484B). As we have already seen in Erasmus' discussion of the Hesiodic proverb about halves and wholes, Plato and his contemporaries called this taking more than one's fair share *pleonexia*; and, as we have also seen, *pleonexia* stands in direct opposition to *isotēs* or equality, the principle at the root not only of justice, as Plato understands it, but of such related quali-

10. On this adage see Erasmus, *Adages*, I.ix.52, LB, II, 353DE; *CWE*, 32, 210; II.ix.52, LB, II, 674D-675A; *CWE*, 34, 110 and compare I.iii.97 — *septem convivium, novem convicium* — where the similarity in sound of the Latin for "feast" and "fight" reinforces the sense, and also III.i.17, LB, II, 721BC, *CWE*, 34, 188–89. See also Plato, *Gorgias*, ed. E.R. Dodds (Oxford, 1959), 188 and Seth Benardete, *The Rhetoric of Morality and Philosophy: Plato's "Gorgias" and "Phaedrus"* (Chicago, 1991), 8–9.

On the agonistic elements—the dialogue as *machē*—see, for instance, 339E; for the culinary aspect—the dialogue as *eortē*—see 464D-465A. Both features are traditional. See also Michel Jeanneret, *A Feast of Words: Banquets and Table Talk in the Renaissance*, trans. Jeremy White and Emma Hughes (Chicago, 1991).

ties as *taxis* and *kosmos*.[11] Indeed, the *aretē* or excellence of political *koinōnia*, like that of the human *psychē*, depends on these very qualities. Here as in the *Republic* Socrates constructs the analogy between the well-ordered city and the well-ordered soul on the basis of their common characteristics (504AD, 506DE, 507D). The individual who lacks these qualities will inevitably be incapable of taking part appropriately in the life of the community (507E-508A):

> For neither to any of his fellowmen can such a one be dear (*prosphilēs*), nor to God; since he cannot commune (*koinōnein*) with any, and where there is no communion (*koinōnia*), there can be no friendship (*philia*). And wise men tell us, Callicles, that heaven and earth and gods and men are held together by communion (*koinōnian*) and friendship (*philian*), by orderliness (*kosmiotēta*), temperance, and justice; and that is the reason, my friend, why they call the whole (*to holon*) of this world by the name of order (*kosmon*), not of disorder or dissoluteness. Now you, as it seems to me, do not give proper attention to this, for all your cleverness, but have failed to observe the great power of geometrical equality (*hē isotēs hē geōmetrikē*) amongst both gods and men:

11. On the Pythagorean origin of the related concepts of *kosmos, taxis, philia*, and *koinōnia*, see C. J. De Vogel, *Pythagoras and Early Pythagoreanism* (Assen, 1966), 104-05, 116-19 and 192-218; E. R. Dodds, 337-40; Jean-Claude Fraisse, *La notion d'amitié dans la philosophie antique* (Paris, 1974), 55-67.

For the Pythagoreanism of the *Gorgias*, including the parable, see Dodds, 20, 296-98 and J. S. Morrison, "Pythagoras of Samos," *Classical Quarterly*, n.s. 6 (1956), 135-56 and "The Origins of Plato's Philosopher-Statesman," *Classical Quarterly*, n.s. 8 (1958), 198-218.

> you hold that self-advantage (*pleonexian*) is what
> one ought to practice, because you neglect geometry
> (*geōmetrias*).

In keeping with his views about subordinating philosophical education to political ambition, Callicles himself lacks the intellectual training that would prepare him to appreciate either these underlying commonalities or their consequences for living the best life.

Instead, in the company of his friends—the so-called *koinōnia sophias* or "wise-guys club" (487B)—Callicles spends his time considering just how much philosophy the politician needs. Consequently, he neglects the teachings of another group of "wise guys," the Pythagoreans, whose students, on the contrary, spend their time learning to recognize in themselves and the world *kosmos, taxis* and *isotēs*. For the Pythagoreans, whose parable of the ordered life or *kosmios bios* Socrates invokes (493A–494A), understand the universe or cosmos itself to be held together by an attractive force or *philia* that binds not only mortal creatures to one another, but mortal to immortal in correspondence with a model of mathematics that is rooted in turn in these principles.[12] Callicles' misguided pursuit of rhetoric as popularly

---

12. See De Vogel, p. 194: "It is clear that the Wise men referred to are the Pythagoreans. Their cosmic and universal thought is used by Socrates-Plato as the very basis of the doctrine of man's social existence just as they had always done themselves. Human virtue must be an imitation of cosmic harmony; the principle of order implies restraint of desires and therefore unity, justice, inward peace and happiness. Thus the Pythagorean ethic inspires Plato's social ethic; we find its elaboration in the *Republic* finally confirmed in the *Laws*.

The principle of geometric equality, which not only occurs in this place in the *Gorgias* but is the leading principle in the *Republic*, where democracy is branded as the greatest injustice since it wishes to apply an *arithmetic* equality, may be found in Archytas, fr. 2."

practiced, instead of philosophy, follows like all wrong action from ignorance, and specifically from ignorance of Pythagorean discipline, including mathematics. Even the rhetorician, if properly trained, invests his compositions with these qualities (503E–504A).

Unschooled in the doctrines of Pythagoras, Callicles not surprisingly also misunderstands the relation between the politician and his audience. For it too, Socrates claims, derives from an old Pythagorean saying: like to like (510B).[13] Only by really befriending (*eis philian*) the Athenian people—that is, only by becoming profoundly like them—can any politician hope to persuade them (513B; cf. *Laws* 716B–717D). After much argumentation, in other words, Socrates returns to a claim advanced much earlier in the dialogue with his first interlocutor. Far from being an art or *technē* grounded in knowledge of a subject matter, rhetoric is a kind of know-how, an *empeiria*, by which the ignorant gratify others like themselves (462C, 465A; cf. 448C). "So he who does not know," Socrates puts the case to Gorgias at the outset, "will be more convincing to those who do not know than he who knows" (459B).

Without explicitly alluding to the Pythagorean proverb about friendship and common property, as we have seen, the *Gorgias* characterizes its own rhetorical and political theory, in stark contrast to that both practiced and preached by Gorgias and Callicles, as grounded in the Pythagorean principle of *koinōnia*

13. See also 507E, *Phaedrus* 240C and 255B, *Lysis* 214B and Dodds, 344. Erasmus notes the adage (I.ii.21) as *homoion homoiōi philon* (LB, II, 79E–80A). Although Erasmus doesn't mention Pythagoras on this particular occasion, this adage is related to *amicitia aequalitas*, the second of the *Pythagorae symbola* (LB, II, 14F–15C). See in addition Aristotle, *Nicomachean Ethics*, trans. H. Rackham, LCL (Cambridge, Mass., 1926; rpt. 1975), 8.8.5: "Amity consists in equality (*isotēs*) and similarity (*homoiōtēs*), especially the similarity of those who are alike in virtue."

and its attendant qualities of *taxis* and *kosmos*. In addition to incorporating an elaborate myth of psychic migration that boldly advertises Plato's pedigree in the earlier Italian school, this dialogue also betrays its Pythagorean heritage in its reliance on proverbial statement, and especially on proverbs about friendship.[14] Alongside this legacy of myth and proverb, moreover, it inherits the Pythagorean homology between politics, rhetoric and theology, an homology rooted in a cosmic *philia*, rooted in turn in *koinōnia*. Fully appreciating the commonalities between the right kind of rhetorical and philosophical training or *askēsis*, Socrates nevertheless subordinates practicing rhetoric (*askountes rhētorikēn*) to practicing virtue (*askountes aretēn*) (500C, 527DE).[15]

Whereas the *Gorgias*, as one of the two Platonic dialogues explicitly concerned with rhetoric, begins with a proverb, the *Phaedrus*, as the other, ends with one, and more precisely with our Pythagorean proverb. Phaedrus himself invokes the adage, moreover, in response to Socrates' closing prayer for *philia* or friendship between the inner and outer man, between his intellectual store and his material possessions—only such wealth, Socrates prays, as the self-possessed man, the *sōphrōn*, can handle (279C). Hoping for a full share in the prayer of his *philos* or friend, Phaedrus' amen takes proverbial form: friends hold all things (including their prayers) in common.[16]

14. On the Pythagorean origins of these myths of psychic migration see Iamblichus, *De vita pythagorica,* 179; De Vogel, 192–93 and Dodds, 297–99.

15. On the difference between ancient and medieval *askēsis* or "asceticism" see Pierre Hadot, *Philosophy as a Way of Life,* trans. Michael Chase (Oxford, 1995), 128. See also Mary Carruthers, *The Craft of Thought,* 106–08. I will return to this topic below.

16. Among the other well-known proverbs in this dialogue are "Friendship is equality" and "A friend is another self," both featured

Phaedrus' call for commonality in friendship in response to Socrates' final prayer to Pan echoes Socrates' earlier prayer to Erōs as *philos* (257A) at the end of his palinode. This prayer, not incidentally, calls for Lysias' conversion to the philosophical life (257B). Aimed directly at the orator, however, Socrates' protreptic actually targets Phaedrus, who, the philosopher understands all too well, will imitate his much-admired model for better or for worse (257B, Cobb, 113):[17]

> If Phaedrus and I said anything harsh about you in the earlier speech, blame Lysias as the father of that speech. Make him cease from such speeches and turn him toward friendship with wisdom, as his brother Polemarchus has been turned, so that his lover here will no longer be ambivalent, as he is now, but rather will dedicate his life entirely to love through speeches that are characterized by friendship with wisdom.

---

among the *Pythagorae symbola* that follow the opening adage (I.i.2, LB, II, 14F-15C, *CWE*, 31, 31), "The sweet elbow" (*Phaedrus* 257E, II.i.38, LB, II, 419F-420E, *CWE*, 33, 37-39), "The shadow of an ass" (*Phaedrus* 260C, I.iii.52, LB, II, 132C-133D, *CWE*, 31, 278-80) and "The garden of Adonis" (*Phaedrus* 276B, I.i.4, LB, II, 26C-27B, *CWE*, 31, 51-53).

On the *Phaedrus*, and especially its treatment of *philia*, see *Plato's Erotic Dialogues*, trans. with commentary William S. Cobb (Albany, 1993), 169-70; Eden, " 'Between Friends All is Common': The Erasmian Adage and Tradition," 405-19; Fraisse, 158-67; Charles L. Griswold, *Self-Knowledge in Plato's "Phaedrus"* (New Haven, 1986).

17. On Phaedrus' misguided use of imitation in place of the deeper relation of similarity, see Eden, " 'Between Friends All is Common': The Erasmian Adage and Tradition," 413-14. For later treatments of this distinction in the Platonic tradition see Wesley Trimpi, *Muses of One Mind: The Literary Analysis of Experience and Its Continuity* (Princeton, 1983), 164-240.

Unlike his full participation in Socrates' closing prayer, in other words, Phaedrus' amen here is contingent, and for the very reasons that Socrates has just disclosed. Phaedrus has yet to choose between the life of *philosophia* and that of *philotimia*—between Socrates and Lysias. Indeed, Phaedrus himself identifies the much-imitated Lysias as a *philotimos*, one who writes or refrains from writing as reputation demands (257C).[18]

Like the *Protagoras*, the *Gorgias*, and the *Symposium*, then, the *Phaedrus* takes as a point of departure the *agōn* between competing ways of life, a competition traditionally associated with Pythagoras. Like the *Gorgias*, moreover, the *Phaedrus* fortifies this Pythagorean association through its myth of psychic migration. Shaping Socrates' second, recantatory speech, this myth elaborates the rewards and punishments attending the choices we make concerning the kinds of lives we live—lives ranging from the philosophical to the tyrannical (248DE). In particular, Socrates' myth features the very choice facing not only Phaedrus but presumably also many of Plato's earliest readers.

For only the soul that consistently chooses the life of *philosophia* finally escapes the repetition of judgment and reembodiment (248E–249A). Only these *philosophoi* prevail in the ferocious psychological struggles that threaten the orderly life —the *kosmios bios* (256AB). The *philotimoi*, on the other hand, often through what Socrates calls *ameleia* or carelessness (256C), succumb to their baser impulses, thus straining the integrity of a relation characterized almost indifferently as friendship or love (256CD):

> These two [i.e. the *philotimoi*] are also friends, then, though less so than the other pair [i.e. the *philosophoi*], and remain together both while they are

18. For the poet Simonides as similarly *philotimos*, see *Protagoras* 343C.

in love and after love has departed, for they believe they have each given and received the strongest
vows, which it would be unlawful to break by ever
becoming enemies.

Like the *Symposium,* in other words, the *Phaedrus* asks us to consider not only the relation between *erōs* and *logos,* as students
of Plato regularly note, but also that between *erōs* and *philia.*[19]
Whereas Socrates' recantatory second speech sets in high relief the commonalities between friendship and love, Socrates'
first speech challenges Lysias' oration on behalf of the nonlover
without challenging its underlying assumption, to the contrary,
of an antagonism or enmity between friendship and love. And
Socrates' demonstration of this antagonism assumes with the
Pythagorean adage the holding in common of friendship.

For if friendship presumes both commonality and equality,
lovers by contrast—at least in Socrates' first speech—deprive
their beloveds of property and even other friends in an effort
to ensure their inferiority and continued dependence (239E–
240A). More damaging still, these same lovers turn their be-

19. Indeed, as Socrates formulates the question under debate in the
first part of the dialogue (237C), it is "whether one should enter into a
friendship with one who loves or with one who does not" (Cobb, 96).

See, for instance, G. J. de Vries, *A Commentary on the "Phaedrus" of
Plato* (Amsterdam, 1969), 22–24; G. R. F. Ferrari, *Listening to the Cicadas:
A Study of Plato's "Phaedrus"* (Cambridge, 1987); Griswold, *Self-Knowledge
in Plato's "Phaedrus,"* 138–201; Horst Hutter, *Politics as Friendship: The
origins of classical notions of politics in the theory and practice of friendship*
(Waterloo, Ontario, 1978), 64–102; Paul Plass, "The Unity of the *Phae-
drus,*" *Symbolae Osloenses,* 43 (1968), 7–38; rpt. *Plato: True and Sophistic
Rhetoric,* ed. Keith V. Erickson (Amsterdam, 1979), 193–221.

For another reading of the reciprocity between lovers idealized in
the *Phaedrus,* see Helene Foley, "'The Mother of the Argument': *Eros
and the Body in Sappho and Plato's *Phaedrus,*" *Parchments of Gender:
Deciphering the Bodies of Antiquity,* ed. Maria Wyke (Oxford, 1998), 39–70.

loveds away from the philosophical life, discouraging their "divine friendship with wisdom" (239B). This apotreptic intention is in direct conflict with Socrates' openly stated hopes for Phaedrus noted above (cf. 261A). Unlike the friend who freely shares his aspirations for intellectual progress, the so-called left-handed lover selfishly guards against any such progress for his beloved (cf. 266A).

The lover of Socrates' first speech, then, behaves in starkest opposition to the Pythagorean adage. The so-called right-handed lover of the palinode, in contrast, enacts the code of conduct proverbially endorsed. Not only does he not deprive the beloved of material property and social intercourse with other friends, but he himself grows neglectful of his own possessions and even of other people, so complete and sufficient is his association with the beloved—an association that Socrates, as we have already seen, characterizes most emphatically as *philia* or friendship. So Socrates insists that (255B)

> it is fated that bad is never to be a friend (*philon*) to bad nor good not to be a friend (*philon*) to good. When he has accepted the lover and enjoyed his conversation and his company, the goodwill of the lover that is revealed in their close relationship amazes the beloved, and he discovers that all his other friends and relatives offer no friendship (*philias*) at all in comparison with this friend who is divinely inspired.

Bound to one another through a profound likeness or similarity, lover and beloved find equality in a friendship that both surpasses any they have ever experienced and endures throughout their lives (255E, 256CE).

Unquestionably about *erōs* and *logos* and arguably about *erōs* and *philia*, the *Phaedrus* is also, I would suggest, about *logos* and *philia,* which at their best or most excellent share a commitment to *koinōnia* or commonality. For like friends after the Pythagorean fashion, discourse in the form of speaking, writing and even thinking assumes not only as its own standard of excellence the criterion of unity or wholeness (264C) but also in relation to its subject matter the task of apprehending what seemingly disparate things have in common. Suffering, like everyone else, from love-sickness, Socrates confesses his peculiar erotic attachment not only to this process of searching out such commonalities but even to those who practice the search most philosophically; and not, we can infer, in order to imitate them, as Phaedrus aspires to imitate Lysias, but rather in order to become profoundly like them, in the deeper philosophical sense of sharing their company (266BC):[20]

> I, myself, Phaedrus, am a lover (*erastēs*) of these dividings and collectings as what enable me to speak and to think, and when I believe that someone else is able to see the natural unity and plurality of things, I follow him, "walking behind him in his footsteps as

20. On the distinction between imitation and similarity, see above n. 17. On the role of *koinōnia* in discourse see *Gorgias* 464C and *Statesman,* trans. Harold N. Fowler, LCL (Cambridge, Mass., 1925; rpt. 1975), 285AB: "because people are not in the habit of considering things by dividing them into classes, they hastily put these widely different relations into the same category, thinking they are alike; and again they do the opposite of this when they fail to divide other things into parts. What they ought to do is this: when a person at first sees only the unity or common quality (*koinōnian*) of many things, he must not give up until he sees all the differences in them, so far as they exist in classes; and conversely, when all sorts of dissimilarities are seen in a large number of objects he must find it impossible to be discouraged or to stop until he has gathered into one circle of similarity (*homoiōtētos*) all the things which are related to each other and has included them in some sort of class on the basis of their essential nature." And see de Vries, 218–19.

in those of a god." Moreover, up to now, I've called those who're able to do this dialecticians, though whether I address them correctly or not only a god knows.

And while the activity of apprehending commonality in multiplicity characterizes in particular the kind of discourse belonging to the philosophical life (261E, 265DE, 273D; cf. 259AB, 259E–260A), such apprehensions exercised even intermittently and more or less at random mark us as human (249BC). Whereas the *Symposium*, as we have seen, locates our humanity in our desire for the immortality we lack, the *Phaedrus*, frequently read as its companion piece, takes our immortality as given (245C), defining our humanity instead in terms of this peculiar cognitive process—a process that we hold in common with divinity (247DE).[21]

If remembering activates the kind of knowing we share with the gods, moreover, then the failure to remember that characterizes the *ameleia* or negligence of the *philotimoi* poses the gravest threat to living philosophically (248CE).[22] So threatening to his philosophical agenda does Socrates find this negligence or carelessness—what he calls at the end of the *Phaedrus ameletēsia* (275A)—that he denies that writing is a philosophically serious practice precisely because it fosters this condition.

The opposite of *ameleia* and *ameletēsia*, on the other hand, is *meletē*, often translated as "practice"; and *meletē* figures promi-

21. At 245C Socrates associates the immortality of the soul with its perpetual motion. Aristotle attributes this theory of the soul's immortality to the Pythagorean Alcmaeon (*De anima*, 405a30).

22. At 259BD Socrates invokes the myth of the cicadas both as a warning against the dangers of *ameleia* and as an exhortation to the practice of philosophical discourse rewarded by Calliope and Urania. See ch. 2, n. 13. On Pythagorean anxiety over this threat see de Vries, 142.

nently, as we have seen, in Diotima's account of how human knowing can approach the stability and continuity of divine knowing. It also comprises the third ingredient with natural talent (*physis*) and knowledge (*epistēmē*) that, according to Socrates in conversation with Phaedrus, goes into making the consummate rhetorician (269D). When Socrates meets Phaedrus outside the city's walls, the would-be orator is engaged in just this kind of practice or *meletē* with Lysias' speech (228B).[23]

As Plato's other dialogue about rhetoric, then, the *Phaedrus* advances the conversation of the *Gorgias* by imagining an art or *technē* in place of an artless routine or *atechnos tribē* (260E; cf. 270B), one based not on a haphazard *empeiria* but on a more reflective *meletē*. In the *Phaedrus*, in other words, Socrates makes the case for a rhetorical training that is not only more practicable but also more fully integrated into the philosophical life. As we have seen, the *Gorgias* subordinates the *askēsis* or practice of rhetoric to that of virtue. So does the *Phaedrus*, but it does so while promoting a rhetorical *praxis* supported by a dialectical understanding of both dialectic itself and psychology (271C–272B).

---

23. For the role of *meletē*—Latin, *meditatio*—in the rhetorical tradition see *De oratore* 1.30.136, 1.32.147; Tacitus, *Dialogus de oratoribus*, 16.1, 30.2, 33.5 and Carruthers, *The Craft of Thought*, 105–08. On the study or *meletē* of poetry, especially as it corresponds to Pythagorean and Platonic philosophy, see Plutarch, *Moralia* 35F. For its role in the philosophical tradition as *meditatio* see Pierre Hadot, *Philosophy as a Way of Life*, 59, 84–89 and 112, n. 38: "It is only after much hesitation that I have translated *meletē* by 'meditation.' In fact, *meletē* and its Latin equivalent *meditatio* designate 'preparatory exercises,' in particular those of rhetoricians. If I have finally resigned myself to adopting the translation 'meditation,' it is because the exercise designated by *meletē* corresponds, in the last analysis, rather well to what we nowadays term *meditation:* an effort to assimilate an idea, notion, or principle, and make them come alive in the soul." For its possible early role in Pythagoreanism, see 116, n. 79.

In considering what the rhetorician should know, moreover, the *Phaedrus* looks back to the *Symposium,* where, as we have seen, Eryximachus introduced the competition among the professions for the right to pass on to the next generation through education the "intellectual property" that enables the transformation of souls. Without rehearsing in full the *agōn* of this earlier dialogue, Plato does reengage the problematic of tradition there explored, drawing our attention to its bearing on the question at hand. For in the later dialogue Socrates adduces the testimony of Eryximachus to demonstrate the limitations of passing on a partial inheritance, one that trains the student how to effect certain changes in the body without teaching him when to effect such changes, on whom and why (*Phaedrus* 268AB):

> Well, tell me, if someone came to your associate Eryximachus or to his father Acumenus and said, "I know how to apply certain sorts of things to people's bodies so as to induce warmth or coolness if I want to, and if I choose I can make them vomit or make their bowels move, and a great many other such things; and because I know these things I'm a competent physician and can make a physician out of anyone else to whom I transmit (*paradō*) knowledge of these things." What do you think they'd say if they heard that?

Socrates, in other words, challenges Phaedrus to reflect on a complete as opposed to a partial rhetorical education. At the same time, he challenges his reader to recall Phaedrus' part in an earlier dialogue that addressed the very problematic of handing this knowledge on: what Plato, like those who follow him, will call *paradosis.* In the *Phaedrus,* moreover, Socrates claims that among the things handed down (*paradosein*) is virtue itself (270B).

In the *Protagoras,* on the other hand, Socrates had questioned the sophist's promise to teach virtue. Indeed, he challenges just this aspect of the Protagorean program, calling Pericles to witness. For while the sons can inherit their father's property, his excellence or *aretē* as a citizen among citizens cannot be passed on. "[I]t is not only so with the service of the State (*to koinon tēs poleōs*)," Socrates argues (319E–320A),

> but in private life our best and wisest citizens are unable to transmit (*paradidonai*) this excellence (*aretēn*) of theirs to others; for Pericles, the father of these young fellows here, gave them a first-rate training in the subjects for which he found teachers, but in those of which he is himself a master he neither trains (*paideuei*) them personally nor commits (*paradidosin*) them to another's guidance.

Unconvinced in the *Protagoras* of the sophistic claim that *aretē* can be taught, Socrates does not reject all aspects of sophistic training. Just as Phaedrus studies the works of the orators, including Lysias, and Polus in the *Gorgias* (448E) is assumed to have studied (*memeletēken*) rhetoric, so Socrates, like the sophists and their students, studies poetry. Insofar as *meletē* belongs as much to a sophistic as to a rhetorical education, in other words, Socrates assures Protagoras that he has studied (*memelēkos*) the Simonidean ode under discussion (339B).

Socrates' attention in these dialogues to not only the most valuable way of life but also to the education that enables it brings into focus a training defined by the related activities of *askēsis, meletē* and *paradosis*.[24] Each of these elements, as we have seen, figures prominently in Plato's characterization of the peda-

24. Cf. *Gorgias* 456E and 457C. As we see at *Symposium* 175A, no less a part of this training is withdrawal or *anachōrēsis*.

gogical programs of the sophist and the rhetorician. Each of them, as we have also seen, comes to belong to the training for philosophy as the foundation of the best way of life. And each of them, as we will soon see in chapter 5, figures prominently in the late antique versions of Pythagoreanism, in early Christian *koinōnia,* and in Erasmian *philosophia Christi.* As the institutionalization of ancient *koinōnia,* moreover, cenobitic monasticism, Christianity at its most exalted, inherits not only these elements of the philosophical life but also the proverbial wisdom first attributed to Pythagoras at the very core of communal living: friends holding all things in common. As we will now see in the next chapter, ancient political philosophy contributes no small portion to this inheritance.

4

Property, Pythagoras, and Ancient
Political Philosophy

Advocating a life at once philosophical and Christian in the "Sileni Alcibiadis," Erasmus skillfully anticipates his reader's objection that European princes cannot possibly take Plato's guardians from the *Republic* as their models. In response, Erasmus insists that far from trying to deprive these princes of their wealth, he is rather recommending that they pay more attention to property of another, more valuable kind (LB, II, 777B; *CWE*, 34, 273). In previous chapters, we have already seen that Erasmus inherits his understanding of both friendship and friendship's relation to tradition from a philosophical tradition that goes back to Pythagoras and Plato. In this chapter, we will see that this same philosophical tradition informs Erasmus' understanding of property.

In the opening adage on friendship and property, Erasmus invokes those ancient philosophers most crucial to this understanding: Pythagoras, Plato, Aristotle, and Cicero. As we will see, all four political writers put the issue of property at the very center of their political philosophy. This commonality is far from coincidental, however, in that each of them, beginning with Plato, learns from his predecessors in a continuing tradition, and it is this ancient tradition that Erasmus inherits. So Plato's position on property in both the *Republic* and *Laws* takes its cue from the common ownership of the philosophical community at Croton, while Aristotle's position in the *Politics* modifies a communalism now Platonic as well as Pythagorean. And so Cicero, a student of ancient philosophy, accommodates Greek, especially Platonic, political theory to Roman legal practices and procedures grounded in private property—an accommodation that the author of the *Adages*, in turn, inherits alongside the proverbial wisdom that friends hold all things in common.[1]

Concluding the debate with Thrasymachus while serving as introduction or *prooimion* (357A) to the remaining nine books about justice, the first book of the *Republic* begins with the question of property and more precisely with Socrates' question concerning the status of Cephalus' property as either acquired or inherited (330AB).[2] Both, Cephalus explains: for his grandfather, inheriting from his father about as much as Cephalus now possesses, left vastly more to Cephalus' father, who, losing much of his inheritance, left to Cephalus a substantially diminished

---

1. Whereas Roman law treats *res* or property as one of its three principal subjects, with persons (*de personis*) and actions (*de actionibus*), actually devoting to this member of the triad significantly more than a third of its entire attention, Attic law lacks not only any systematic treatment of property but even a settled term for it. On the difference between Greek and Roman property law see Douglas M. MacDowell, *The Law of Classical Athens* (London, 1978), 132; A. R. W. Harrison, *The Law of Athens: The Family and Property* (Oxford, 1968), 200-01; William Mathie, "Property in the Political Science of Aristotle," *Theories of Property: Aristotle to the Present*, eds. Anthony Parel and Thomas Flanagan (Waterloo, Ontario, 1979), 13-32; Alan Watson, *Legal Transplants: An Approach to Comparative Law*, 2nd Ed. (Athens, Georgia, 1993), 25-28, 75-78.

On the attention to *res* or property in Roman Law, see J. A. C. Thomas, *Textbook of Roman Law* (Amsterdam, 1976), 125: "The largest division of the private law of Rome—taking up Books II and III of Gaius' Institutes and also part of Book IV of those of Justinian—is the law relating to things, *res*."

2. See Harrison, 125 and 233. On the relation of book 1 to the rest of the dialogue see Charles H. Kahn, "Proleptic Composition in the *Republic*, or Why Book 1 was never a Separate Dialogue," *Classical Quarterly*, 43 (1993), 131-42.

estate. Through his own business acumen, Cephalus now hopes to leave to his own sons an estate worth somewhat more than that bequeathed to his father by his grandfather. And not without good reason. In answer to further questioning from Socrates about the benefit of accumulating property (330D), Cephalus contends that being just depends on having the material resources to pay back what one owes to the gods and other men (331AB).

Among Cephalus' *klēronomoi* or heirs is Polemarchus, who at this point in the dialogue inherits his father's argument. Like his ancestors' inheritance, moreover, this argument also changes value in changing hands (331DE). Building on the traditional (Simonidean) definition of justice as some kind of property transaction (e.g., 332A), Polemarchus reformulates the argument in terms of material advantage or profit (*lusitelein*) (343C)[3] —terms in which, on Polemarchus' account, the just man inevitably sustains heavy losses (343DE). Indeed, Polemarchus introduces his portrait of the just man as the losing partner or *koinōnos* in a joint ownership or *koinōnia*(343D):[4]

> First, in their contracts with one another (*koinōnē-sei*), you'll never find, when the partnership (*koinō-*

---

3. See also 348CE, 354A, 359A, 360D, 392BC, 444E and *Laws* 663D. In the course of the *Republic*, Socrates will shift from this term for profit to another, less overtly materialistic term: *ophelein*. Of course, this shift as part of a general movement away from materialism underlies the Socratic argument of this dialogue as a whole.

4. On *koinōnia* as a legal term see Harrison, 239–43, esp. 240: "It is of its essence that the thing owned—usually, but not exclusively, a landed estate—is owned as a whole by the joint owners and not in proportions varying as between one and another of them."

The same Polemarchus who makes this argument for injustice eventually becomes a lover of wisdom, as we learn in the *Phaedrus* (257B).

nias) ends, that a just partner has got more than an
unjust one, but less.

And this is so because the unjust man, in contrast, approaches all
property transactions claiming more than his fair share (*pleonek-
tein*) (344A; cf. 349C, 362B). Both the partnership or *koinōnia*
that comes to characterize the ideal *polis* and the vice that most
jeopardizes its proper functioning, namely *pleonexia*, are rooted,
as the *Adages* records, in notions of property (see 368B-369E,
371B; cf. *Laws* 906C). In the political arena or life of the *polis*,
moreover, the quintessential unjust man, according to Polemarchus, is the tyrant, characterized in the first book of the *Republic*
as one who not only misappropriates the property of the other
citizens but also enslaves these same citizens, making them his
property too (344AB).[5]

Given the focus of the discussion in book 1 on property, Socrates reasonably excludes his guardians, whose rule is antitheti-
cal to the tyrant's, from all private ownership. If tyranny, as the
greatest possible deterioration of political life, eventually takes
all of the city's resources, including its citizens, as its own private property, rulers of the most excellent political partnership
or *koinōnia*, at the other extreme, own nothing at all. Holding
everything, including their women and children, in common
(*koinōnia gynaikōn te kai paidōn*), the guardians form an association on the model of the paradigmatic *koinōnia*—friendship
or *philia*. So Socrates justifies their peculiar social organization
with an invocation in book 4 of the well-known proverb about
friendship (423E-424A):

5. See also 568DE. On that form of government called oligarchy or
timocracy and based on property ownership, see 550CD, 553C-554B, *Laws*
832C and Seth Benardete, *Socrates' Second Sailing: On Plato's "Republic"*
(Chicago, 1989), 194-98. On tyranny, see Benardete, 203-07.

for if by being well educated [the guardians] become reasonable men, they will easily see these things for themselves, as well as all the other things we are omitting, for example, that marriage, the having of wives, and the procreation of children must be governed as far as possible by the old proverb: Friends possess everything in common (*koina ta philōn*).

And so Adeimantus comes back to this same proverb in book 5, calling for a more extended treatment of the most peculiar aspects of its political application (449C):

We think that you're slacking off and that you've cheated us out of a whole important section of the discussion in order to avoid having to deal with it. You thought we wouldn't notice when you said—as though it were something trivial—that, as regards wives and children, anyone could see that the possessions of friends should be held in common (*koina ta philōn*).

Furthermore, if the guardians apply this first principle of friendship to every aspect of their social organization, the tyrant, at the other extreme, never experiences any friendship at all—not even the garden variety kind (576A). Unfriended, the tyrant is also unjust (*adikos*) (576A); for justice, as Socrates has established earlier with Thrasymachus in book 1, is the basis of *homonoia* or likemindedness and *philia* (351D).[6]

6. For the proverb about the attraction of like to like see 329A, 349D, 350C, 401D, 425C and *Laws* 716C, 728B, 837AB. For other proverbs see 341C, 362D, 377A, 435C, 453A, 492E, 493D, 497E, 544E, 550D, 563C.

See also Horst Hutter, *Politics as Friendship: The origins of the classical notions of politics in the theory and politics of friendship* (Waterloo, Ontario, 1978), 91–102.

In taking friendship as its model, the *koinōnia* or partnership formed by the guardians evokes both our proverb that friends hold all things in common and also the traditional source of this proverb—Pythagoras. Indeed, the guardians' training, so crucial as we have seen in the quotation above to the success of their social organization, is a Pythagorean training, one that teaches them, among other things, to honor gods, parents, and friends (386A), to embrace the doctrine of psychic migration and, especially significant for my argument, to both practice and preach a radical theory of property.[7] As tradition records (and as we will

7. In addition to these elements and the Pythagorean adages already introduced that inform the argument as a whole, other Pythagorean elements include *koinobios* or the common life (458CD) and the teachings about music and astronomy (530D). On the teachings of Pythagoras, including his political philosophy, see Kurt von Fritz, *Pythagorean Politics in Southern Italy* (New York, 1940); S. K. Heninger, Jr., *Touches of Sweet Harmony: Pythagorean Cosmology and Renaissance Poetics* (San Marino, Calif., 1974); Hutter, 48–55; J. S. Morrison, "Pythagoras of Samos," *Classical Quarterly*, n.s. 6 (1956), 135–56; J. A. Philip, *Pythagoras and Early Pythagoreanism* (Toronto, 1966); C. J. De Vogel, *Pythagoras and Early Pythagoreanism* (Assen, 1966). And see my *"Koinōnia* and the Friendship between Rhetoric and Religion," *Rhetorical Invention and Religious Inquiry*, eds. W. Jost and W. Olmsted (New Haven, 2000), 305–22.

For the influence of Pythagoras on Plato's political theory see E. Barker, *The Political Thought of Plato and Aristotle* (New York, 1959), 19–22 and 137–63, esp. 22: "the history of the Pythagorean club might suggest to Plato the rule of philosopher kings. It is certain that Pythagorean ideas were vigorous in Plato's time. Thebes had come under their influence: the Pythagorean Lysis was the instructor of Epaminondas, who called him father; and Aristotle tells us that at Thebes, 'as soon as the rulers became philosophers, the city began to flourish.' Archytas of Tarentum was a famous Pythagorean of the fourth century, who for a long time was supreme in his native city, and served seven times as its general, in spite of a law to the contrary. A man like Archytas, general of his city, and also teacher of philosophy to his disciples in his garden-precinct at Tarentum must obviously have served as a model for the *Republic*, even

see in more detail in the following chapter), Pythagoras organized his commune at Croton on the principle of all things in common as the only basis for a fair and just society.[8] *Koinōnia* as commonality in the material (or we might say economic) sense, in other words, lays the ground for *koinōnia* in the intellectual or psychological sense as community. In fact, Pythagoreans attend to the details of material well-being as a necessary scaffolding for the leisure that allows even greater attention to their intellectual or spiritual provision. And this hierarchy of intellectual above material needs leaves its mark not only on the *Republic* but on all of Plato's writings.

Shortly before the closing discussion of psychic migration—the so-called myth of Er—in a passage already quoted at the opening of chapter 2, Plato has Socrates single out both the *vita pythagorica*, the Pythagorean way of life, as worthy of approbation, and Pythagoras, its founder, as more praiseworthy than Homer (600AB). In keeping with this approval, the citizens of Plato's ideal city embrace the *vita pythagorica* in a number of respects, and not least in the organization of its rulers. Like the

---

if the original club under Pythagoras was not present to Plato's mind. When we remember that Archytas was living at Tarentum, and Epaminondas at Thebes, in the very days when Plato wrote, the *Republic* begins to assume a decidedly practical aspect." Shorey, on the other hand, takes a less appreciative view of the Pythagorean influence, suggesting that "[t]he student of Plato will do well to turn the page when he meets the name Pythagoras in a commentator" (189, n.f). And see F. M. Cornford, *The Republic of Plato* (London, 1941; rpt. 1968), xxvi-xxvii and J. S. Morrison, "The Origins of Plato's Philosopher-Statesman," *Classical Quarterly*, n.s. 8 (1958), 198–218.

8. See, for instance, Iamblichus, *On the Pythagorean Life*, trans. Gillian Clark (Liverpool, 1989), 29–30 and 167–68, where the late antique schoolmaster attributes Plato's communalism in the *Republic* to Pythagoras. And see Edwin J. Minar, "Pythagorean Communism," *Transactions and Proceedings of the American Philological Association*, 75 (1944), 34–46.

initiates at Croton, the guardians pursue a happiness unthinkable to the likes of Adeimantus (419E), a happiness without ownership. Like the Pythagoreans but unlike Socrates' interlocutors in this dialogue, Plato's guardians are content to say "'mine' and 'not mine' of the same things in the same way" (462D; see 462B–464C).

In the *Laws*, Plato's last work, the Athenian stranger reinvests the *Republic*'s positive political values of *philia* and *koinōnia* (708C, 730E, 837AB)—values epitomized in the Pythagorean proverb about friends holding all things in common. Indeed, Plato has his Athenian recall both the proverb and the city of the *Republic* fashioned after these values (739BD; cf. 807B):[9]

> That State and polity come first, and those laws are best, where there is observed as carefully as possible throughout the whole State the old saying that "friends have all things really in common" (*koina ta philōn*). As to this condition,—whether it anywhere exists now, or ever will exist,—in which there is community of wives, children, and all chattels (*koina de chrēmata xumpanta*), and all that is called "private" (*idion*) is everywhere and by every means rooted out of our life . . . no one will ever lay down another definition that is truer or better than these conditions in point of super-excellence.

9. Plato, *The Laws*, trans. R. G. Bury, LCL (Cambridge, Mass., 1926; rpt. 1967), 2 vols. On the relation of the *Laws* to the *Republic*, see Barker, 185–207; David Cohen, "Law, Autonomy and Political Community in Plato's *Laws*," *Classical Philology*, 88 (1993), 301–17; André Laks, "Legislation and Demiurgy: On the Relationship Between Plato's *Republic* and *Laws*," *Classical Antiquity*, 9 (1990), 209–29; Paul Shorey, "Plato's *Laws* and Unity of Plato's Thought," *Classical Philology*, 9 (1914), 345–69; R. F. Stalley, *An Introduction to "Plato's Laws"* (London, 1983), 8–22.

Plato also has the Athenian stranger recall those polities realized in time and place that fell short of these values. As historical instances he offers the Egyptians and Phoenicians (747BC; cf. *Republic* 436A), both ruined by their love of property or *philochrēmatia*. For the aim of establishing and preserving cities, he insists, is not the accumulation of property, which divides citizens from one another, but the fostering of fellowship or *philia* (742D, 743C), which unites them. Another example is Persia (695C-697D), which thrived so long as the feelings of *philia* and *koinōnia* united the people under Darius (695D), deteriorating as these same feelings deteriorated under Xerxes (697CD).[10]

The *Laws*, then, not only reinvests the *Republic*'s political values of *philia* and *koinōnia* but does so by setting them off against the more material value of property. On the other hand, the *Laws* retreats from the *Republic*'s wholesale rejection of private property, settling for the second best polity, one in which property, while still not the aim of political life (743CE), is nonetheless vigorously protected by law (739E-742C). Pursuing the *Republic*'s analogy between *polis* and *psychē* — city and soul — the later dialogue moreover finds a common ground between politics and psychology in this notion of private property.[11] As characterized by the Athenian stranger at the opening of book 5, the soul itself is not only property or *ktēma* but the most inalienable — *oikeiōteron* — of properties (726E, 731C).[12]

10. See Stalley, 76-79.

11. Cf. *Laws* 689AB and 714A and Laks, 221.

12. For a sharper distinction in this passage between property that is private and property that is inalienable see Leo Strauss, *The Argument and the Action of Plato's Laws* (Chicago, 1975), 75: "We have heard previously that the soul is in the highest degree a man's own (726a2-3); but this does not mean that the soul is private; one's own is opposed to the alien or alienable (cf. Thucydides I 70.6), while the private is opposed to the

In keeping with the inalienability of one's own soul, the *Laws* upholds as one of its guiding principles the inviolability more generally of the individual's right to his property (737AD, 739E–740B).[13] Following an extended *prooimion* lasting over four books (734E), the laws themselves begin with the equitable distribution of property among the citizens (736D–737D), thus adding equity or *epieikeia* to the political virtues of *koinōnia* and *philia*.[14]

---

public or common. Thoughts are by nature common—as common as the truth—not private, though they may be accidentally private. The soul is not the self, i.e., the man himself; the man himself is the soul and the body (cf. the first word of the *Phaedo*)."

But see Glenn R. Morrow, *Plato's Cretan City: A Historical Interpretation of the "Laws"* (Princeton, 1960; rpt. 1993), 107: "Plato's institution does not fit any of our familiar conceptions, but it can best be described as private ownership, subject to very special controls that Plato thinks necessary in the interests of the family and the state. These latter interests take precedence in a moral sense over those of the individual, but the legal responsibility for the proper use, maintenance, and control of the land lies with the persons who at any given time are recognized as lot holders."

13. On the other hand, this right to property extends to the owner only during his lifetime, for the reasons articulated in this direct address by the legislator to property-owners concerning inheritance (923AC): "O friends, we will say, for you, who are literally but creatures of a day, it is hard at present to know your own possessions, and the Pythian oracle declares, your own selves, to boot. So I, as lawgiver, make this ruling—that both you yourself and this your property are not your own but belong to the whole of your race, both past and future, and that still more truly does all your race (*to genos*) and its property (*tēn ousian*) belong to the State; and this being so, I will not willingly consent if anyone persuades you to make a will contrary to what is best, by fawning on you and helping you when afflicted by disease or age; rather will I legislate with a general view to what is best for your whole race and State, justly accounting of minor importance the interest of the individual."

14. Strauss makes this point (72): "The question regarding the composition of the citizen body and the question regarding property are the fundamental questions concerning the regime. They are the fundamental political questions and cannot be classified as social in contradistinction

Departing further from the *Republic* but fully in keeping with this distribution, the city's laws recognize distinctions among its citizens according to their property holdings, ranking them in one of four classes (744C–745B).[15]

Taking property distribution as its point of departure in book 5, the *Laws* then returns to matters of property transactions in book 11, which opens by way of recapitulation with a simple rule concerning the inviolability of property (913A):

> So far as possible, no one shall touch my goods
> (*chrēmatōn*) nor move them in the slightest degree,
> if he has in no wise at all got my consent; and I must
> act in like manner regarding the goods of all other
> men, keeping a prudent mind.

Among the transactions covered in book 11 is the transfer of property, which the Athenian proposes to regulate as follows (915CD):

> If anyone claims as his own the beast of any other
> man, or any other of his chattels (*chrēmatōn*), the

---

to political, to make use for the moment of an un-Platonic distinction. Accordingly, the Athenian devotes the rest of Book Five to these two questions." See also Paul Friedlaender, *Plato: An Introduction* (Princeton, 1958; rpt. 1969), 303–07 and Morrow, 101–38.

On equity and its relation to political justice, introduced not incidentally by the Pythagorean proverb on friendship and equality, see 757AC.

15. See Morrow, 134: "It is one of Plato's striking departures from Athenian law to constitute his council by property classes instead of by tribes." On the other hand, Morrow continues (137), "it is not used to deny the poorer classes access to this body but merely to provide equal representation to all property classes. The council in Plato's state, moreover, will be less powerful than the corresponding body at Athens. Above it are the guardians of the laws, in whose selection property qualifications play no part."

man who holds it shall refer the matter to the person who, as being its substantial and lawful owner, sold it or gave it, or made it over (*paradonta*) to him in some other valid way; and this he shall do within thirty days, if the reference be made to a citizen or metic in the city, or, in the case of a foreign delivery (*paradosin*), within five months, of which the middle month shall be that which includes the summer solstice.

Here called *paradosis* by the Athenian, the transfer of property concerns the legislator not only when the property being handed over is material but also when it is intellectual. For education, the political mechanism for handing down intellectual property, demands regulation or *taxis* no less than business, and so the Athenian expects the legislator to oversee this *paradosis* as well.[16] "We have next to discuss the question of the teaching (*didaskalia*)

---

16. For another instance of *paradosis* as property transfer see 924A.

Throughout the *Laws*, the Athenian emphasizes the need for *taxis*, not only as it concerns the social order in business transactions and education, but also as it underlies the workings of the universe. See, e.g., 966E–968A. On the Pythagorean origins of this emphasis see C. J. De Vogel, *Pythagoras and Early Pythagoreanism*, 104–05, 116–19, 192–218 and Jean-Claude Fraisse, *La notion d'amitié dans la philosophie antique* (Paris, 1974), 55–67.

In *Truth and Method*, Gadamer reasserts the bond between tradition and education (280): "That which has been sanctioned by tradition and custom has an authority that is nameless, and our finite historical being is marked by the fact that the authority of what has been handed down to us—and not just what is clearly grounded—always has power over our attitudes and behavior. All education depends on this, and even though, in the case of education, the educator loses his function when his charge comes of age and sets his own insight and decisions in the place of the authority of the educator, becoming mature does not mean that a person becomes his own master in the sense that he is freed from all tradition."

and imparting (*paradosis*) of these subjects," he asserts in the extended treatment of *paideia* in book 7, "—how, by whom, and when each of them should be practiced" (803A).

The *Laws* follows not only the *Protagoras* and *Phaedrus* in considering both what kind of training is passed on and how but also the *Republic* in fostering the analogy between material and intellectual property. Even without a specialized, legal term for one or the other kind of property, as we have seen, Socrates can toy with Polemarchus' double inheritance (*klēros*) of Cephalus' money and arguments and applaud Pythagoras for handing over (*paredosan*) that constellation of ideas that constitutes the *vita pythagorica*. Leaving behind the *Republic*'s radical theory of property, Plato's final dialogue incorporates once again not only the Pythagorean ethics of friendship and community, regularly formulated in proverbs, but also its cosmology, number theory, and doctrine of psychic migration, especially in books 10 and 12.[17] Indeed, Plato's Athenian is following both Pythagoras and Socrates in subordinating material to intellectual property and in blaming the materialists—those who reduce everything, including divinity, to matter—for the city's ills (886D). On the other hand, the Athenian celebrates education as the means for transferring the intellectual inheritance from one generation of citizens to the next. Like the *Republic*, the *Laws* progresses from a discussion of the disposition of material property to the proper administration of the city's intellectual property.

In keeping with his teacher's political theory, Aristotle's *Politics* begins with the controversial question of property and ends with a discussion of education, insisting that both require careful regulation or *taxis* by the city's laws. Whereas Aristotle outspokenly rejects the notion of common ownership for material

17. See, for instance, 903B–906C and 966C–968B.

property, however, he just as firmly endorses this notion as it pertains to education as the political mechanism, here as in the *Laws,* for the transmission of intellectual property. For it is through a common education or *paideia,* Aristotle claims, rather than through holding property in common, that the *polis* becomes a real community or *koinōnia* (2.2.10).[18]

Indeed, Aristotle introduces his own treatment of property—according to some (2.4.1), the most pressing problem of political theory—with the well-known critique of Plato's solution in the *Republic;* and he does so without completely rejecting the Pythagorean doctrine that underlies this solution. On the contrary, Aristotle follows Plato not only in reciting the Pythagorean proverb about friendship and commonality (2.2.4–5; cf. *Ethics,* 8.9.1–2 and 9.8.2) but also in embracing the political virtues encoded in this proverb. As we learn from the opening sentence of the *Politics, koinōnia* is the essence of *politeia* (1.1.1), while *philia* is the foundation of *koinōnia* (2.1.16, 3.5.14). Aristotle even goes so far as to concede that unity or wholeness is good for political organization or *taxis* provided it is the appropriate unity—one, that is, that allows for multiplicity (2.1.7). For the Socratic hypothesis of unqualified unity as a good for the city misses the mark, Aristotle argues (2.2.9), especially as it characterizes the distribution and ownership of property. Political unity does not follow from citizens saying "mine" and "not mine" about everything (2.1.8).[19] And the principal hindrance to a city so organized is the psychology of its citizens.

18. Compare Isocrates, *Panegyricus* 50, where the term "Hellenes" is said to characterize not those who share a common race—*genos* or *physis*—but a common education or *paideusis.*

19. See Barker, *The Political Thought of Plato and Aristotle,* 231–37; David Konstan, *Friendship in the Classical World* (Cambridge, 1997), 67–82; Martha Craven Nussbaum, "Shame, Separateness, and Politi-

For it is human nature, Aristotle asserts, to love (*philein*) what is one's own (2.1.10, 2.1.17, 2.2.6). Ownership itself, in other words, motivates the *philia* so important to *koinōnia*. So Aristotle replaces Plato's common ownership with private ownership qualified by common use (2.2.5–6, 7.9.6). And so he charges the legislator with overseeing a common education that shapes citizens inclined to share rather than take more than their share. Fostering *koinōnia* instead of *pleonexia* (2.4.6–7; cf. 4.10.5, 5.2.4), in other words, Aristotelian *paideia* looks to equalize (*homalizein*) citizens' desires (*tas epithumias*), not their property (*tas ousias*) (2.4.5).[20]

Rejecting the communism of the *Republic*, as Erasmus records in the 1526 version of the opening adage (see above), Aristotle also disregards the commonalities between divine and human justice that characterize first Pythagorean and then Platonic political philosophy. Perhaps somewhat unexpectedly for its earliest readers, the *Politics* departs from its predecessors in offering no account of psychic migration. Pythagorean in its appreciation of how *taxis* or order grounds *politeia*, *nomos* and even *dikē* itself, Aristotelian political theory not only approaches Pythagorean doctrine more critically but also criticizes Plato for embracing it so unreservedly.[21]

---

cal Unity: Aristotle's Criticism of Plato," *Essays on Aristotle's Ethics,* ed. Amélie Oksenberg Rorty (Berkeley, 1980), 395–435.

20. See Barker, 423–43. On private property with common use see Isocrates, *Areopagiticus* 35 and Alan C. Mitchell, "The Social Foundation of Friendship in Acts 2:44–47 and 4:32–37," *Journal of Biblical Literature,* 111/2 (1992), 255–72, esp. 260–64. See also Hutter, 102–16.

21. For *dikē* defined as *taxis politikēs koinōnias* see 1.1.12; for *taxis* in regard to *nomos*, see 3.11.3 and cf. 7.4.5; and in regard to *politeia*, 4.1.5 and cf. 2.8.1.

For Plato's Pythagoreanism, see especially *Metaphysics* 1.6.1–7, 3.1.13, 3.4.25, 10.2.1. For the Pythagorean roots of Plato's overvaluation of unity

An attentive reader of Greek philosophy, Cicero likewise draws his readers' attention to the Pythagorean elements of Plato's intellectual inheritance; and he does so in a work that itself reinvests the tradition of Platonic political theory (*De re publica*, 1.16):[22]

> Plato traveled first to Egypt for the sake of study, then to Italy and Sicily to learn the discoveries of Pythagoras.... and that since at that time Pythagoras had a great reputation in that region, he devoted himself to the Pythagoreans and their studies. And so, since he loved Socrates above all others and wanted to attribute everything to him, he wove together the wit and subtlety of Socratic conversation with the obscurity of Pythagoras and the weight of his varied erudition.

The *De re publica* is the earliest of Cicero's three political works that bear the mark of both Plato's thinking and its Pythagorean underpinnings; the other two are its companion piece, the *De legibus*, and the *De officiis*. As we shall see, however, all three distance themselves even further than Plato's *Laws* and Aristotle's *Politics* from the radical theory of property that shapes the *Republic*. In contrast to the Athenian philosophers, the Ro-

---

see *Nicomachean Ethics*, 1.6.7. For the Pythagorean tendency to emphasize minor similarities at the expense of more important ones see *Metaphysics* 14.6.4-7. And see Walter Burkert, *Lore and Science in Ancient Pythagoreanism*, 91-92.

22. Cicero, *On the Commonwealth and On the Laws*, ed. James E. G. Zetzel (Cambridge, 1999). For other testimonies to this double intellectual inheritance, see Heninger, *Touches of Sweet Harmony*, 35-36, n. 8. For the revival of Pythagoreanism in Cicero's day see John Dillon, *The Middle Platonists* (London, 1977), 117-21 and Elizabeth Rawson, *Intellectual Life in the Late Roman Republic* (London, 1985), 30-33 and 291-94.

man lawyer-politician approaches this particular subject from the standpoint of Roman law, which takes property, and especially private property, as its own point of departure.

Indeed, Cicero repeatedly characterizes *res publica* in the *De re publica* according to the legal concept of *res,* that is as the property of the people or *res populi;*[23] and like other property or *res* under Roman law, Cicero imagines, the *res publica* should be subject to a legal claim of ownership or *vindicatio* by opposing parties: the people, for instance, against the domination or, in the legal sense, ownership (*dominium*) of a king.[24] On the other

23. See for instance 1.39, 1.41, 1.43, 3.45. On *res* or property in Roman law see J. A. C. Thomas, *Textbook of Roman Law* (Amsterdam, 1976), 125–210; W. W. Buckland, *A Text-book of Roman Law from Augustus to Justinian* (Cambridge, 1921), 182–280; Alan Watson, *The Law of Property in the Later Roman Republic* (Oxford, 1968) and *Roman Private Law around 200 B.C.* (Edinburgh, 1971).

See also Neal Wood, *Cicero's Social and Political Thought* (Berkeley, 1988), 120–42 and Malcolm Schofield, "Cicero's Definition of *Res Publica,*" *Cicero the Philosopher,* ed. J. G. F. Powell (Oxford, 1995), 63–83. While Schofield argues that the law is paradigmatic in Cicero's thinking about politics, he maintains that the model of property operates metaphorically (75). He concludes (82) that "Cicero's treatment of *res publica* has a quite different structure from Platonic and Aristotelian political philosophy, despite his debts to them. What makes the difference is the conceptual framework of Roman law, for it is Roman law which enables questions to be formulated about the rights a free people has to own, lend, transfer, or place in trust powers conceived on the model of property. The Roman legal framework is the common denominator in Cicero's theory of *res populi* and in the later tradition beginning with the formulations of the jurists."

24. See esp. 1.48: "But if the people would maintain their rights, they say that no form of government would be superior, either in liberty or happiness, for they themselves would be [owners] (*domini*) of the laws and the courts, of war and peace, of international agreements, and of every citizen's life and property (*pecuniae*); this government (*rem publicam*) alone, they believe, can rightly be called a commonwealth (*rem*

hand—as Scipio, the principal speaker of this dialogue, argues—
no one person can thus dominate or own a commonwealth or *res
publica*, which by definition represents a partnership or *societas*
(3.43; cf. 1.39).[25] By way of illustration, he offers the historical

---

populi), that is, 'the property of the people.' And it is for that reason, they
say, that 'the property of the people' is often liberated (*vindicari*) from
the domination *(dominatione)* of kings or senators, while free peoples do
not seek kings or the power and wealth of aristocracies." Compare 1.27,
where true ownership or *dominium* belongs only to the wise, who can
claim (*vindicari*) all things as their own according to the law of nature.

On *vindicatio* as a legal action for a claim of ownership see Fritz
Schultz, *Classical Roman Law* (Oxford, 1951), 368: "The classical *rei
vindicatio* was an action by which the plaintiff, on the strength of his
quiritary ownership, demanded the restitution of a thing from the defen-
dant who had the thing in his possession." See also Watson, *The Law of
Property in the Later Roman Republic,* 96–104.

On *dominium* or legal ownership see Schultz, *Roman Republic,* 338–80;
Thomas, 133–34; Watson, *The Law of Property in the Later Roman Republic,* 91–92 and *Rome of the XII Tables: Persons and Property* (Princeton,
1975), 125.

25. On *societas* as a legal partnership, roughly corresponding to the
Greek *koinōnia,* see E. M. Atkins, " 'Domina et Regina Virtutum': Justice
and *Societas* in *De Officiis,*" *Phronesis,* 35 (1990), 258–89; Watson, *Roman
Private Law around 200 B.C.,* 140–43, esp. 140, where he locates the origin of this partnership in cases of inheritance: "Gaius [G.3.154a] tells us
that at one time when a paterfamilias died his *sui heredes* were in a kind of
partnership [societas]—which he describes as *legitima simul et naturalis*—
called *ercto non cito,* that is 'undivided ownership.' Later, other persons
who wished to set up a similar partnership could do so by means of a defi-
nite *legis actio* before the praetor [G.3.154b]." On *ercto non cito,* see below,
p. 113.

See also *Gai institutiones* or *Institutes of Roman Law by Gaius,* trans.
Edward Poste and ed. E. A. Whittuck (Oxford, 1925), III.148: "A partnership (*societatem*) either extends to all the goods (*totorum bonorum*) of
the partners or is confined to a single business, for instance, the purchase
and sale of slaves." And see p. 214, where Whittuck confirms that inheritance law is the paradigm: "Communism or co-ownership appears to be

example of Syracuse, largest and most beautiful of cities but, under Dionysius, no true republic. For the defining feature of a republic, Scipio insists, is not wealth but commonwealth (3.43):

> That great city, which Timaeus says is the greatest of the Greek cities and the most beautiful of all cities — its glorious citadel, its harbor that flows into the center of the town to the foundations of the city itself, its broad streets and porticoes and temples and walls — none of these made it any more of a commonwealth at the time when Dionysius controlled it: nothing belonged to the people, and the people itself belonged to a single man. And so where there is a tyrant, then it is wrong to say, as I did yesterday, that there is a flawed commonwealth: the logic of the argument compels me to say that it is no commonwealth at all.

Like Socrates in the *Republic,* Scipio in the *De re publica* defines the tyrant as one who considers the city, including its citizens, his own private property.[26] Unlike Socrates, however, Sci-

---

an older institution than divided or individual ownership. Even after the rights of the paterfamilias had been enormously developed at the expense of the rest of the household, as may have been the case in prehistoric times, a vestige of the times when property vested rather in the family than in the chief was perhaps preserved in the rules respecting the suus heres. Suus heres appears equivalent to sibi heres, and implies that he who now enters on proprietary rights in the character of paterfamilias had already possessed proprietary rights over the same subject-matter in the character of filiusfamilias."

And see Wood, 138–42. On *socialis* as a translation of *politikos* and the consequences of this translation see Hannah Arendt, *The Human Condition* (Chicago, 1958; rpt. 1989), 22–78.

26. See 2.48: "Who could rightly call 'human' someone who desires no

pio chooses as his exemplary republic one that is both historical and fully committed to private ownership.[27] In keeping with this commitment, the first act of its exemplary ruler, Numa Pompilius, is the distribution of property (2.26). For he understands that political stability depends on the citizens' opportunities to accumulate wealth through the peaceful cultivation of their land instead of the pillage and plunder of their neighbors.[28]

In answer to Manilius' question concerning King Numa's own education, Scipio is especially eager to distance the Roman king from the first philosopher of common property, assuring his friends that tradition notwithstanding Pythagoras traveled through Italy about 150 years after Numa's death (2.28–29).[29] Born too late to influence Numa, according to Scipio, Pythagoras nevertheless figures prominently in the tradition of political discourse that Cicero himself inherits, not only as the father of common property but also as the philosopher of justice, of friendship and of the kind of psychic migration that—recalling

bond (*communionem*) of shared law, no link (*societatem*) of human nature with his fellow citizens or indeed with the whole human race?" And see Schofield, 75.

27. For Cicero on the distinction between his own and Plato's method see *De re publica* 2.3, 2.52 and *De legibus* 1.15, 2.17.

28. Scipio's etymologies set in relief the Roman attention to private property, for "at that time wealth consisted of livestock (*pecus*) and landed property (*loci*), the origin of the words *pecuniosi* and *locupletes* to mean 'wealthy'" (2.16).

29. See also *De oratore*, 2.37.154. Compare Ovid, *Metamorphoses*, 15.1–483 and see Roy Arthur Swanson, "Ovid's Pythagorean Essay," *Classical Journal*, 54 (1958), 21–24. On the Numa forgery of 181 B.C.E. see Holger Thesleff, "An Introduction to the Pythagorean Writings of the Hellenistic Period," *Acta Academiae Aboensis* 24 (1961), 52–53, 98–99.

For Erasmus on Plutarch on the overlap of the projects of Pythagoras and Numa, see LB, II, 15D; *CWE*, 31, 32.

the *Gorgias*, the *Phaedrus* and the *Republic*—structures Scipio's famous dream at the end of the *De re publica* (6.17–29).[30]

In the *De legibus*, Cicero advances not only the treatment of political and legal theory begun in his *De re publica* but also the reinvestment of the Platonic tradition of political discourse informing that work. Placing himself in conversation with his brother Quintus and dearest friend Atticus, he rehearses the special debt of this dialogue to Plato's last work by the same title. "Then is this your wish?" Cicero asks the other two interlocutors (1.15)

> Just as with the Cretan Clinias and the Lacedae-monian Megillus, as [Plato] describes it, he spent a summer day in the cypress groves and forest paths of Cnossos, frequently stopping and occasionally rest-ing, discoursing on public institutions and the best laws, in the same way let us walk and rest among these tall poplars on this green and shady bank and inquire into these same subjects more deeply than is required by the practical uses of the courts.

Obviously indebted to Plato's *Laws*, the *De legibus* also echoes the *Phaedrus*, especially as the conversation begins.

Set, like the *Phaedrus* and the *Laws*, at a distance from city life, this conversation about the best form of a commonwealth

---

30. Cf. 3.19 and *De legibus* 1.33 and 2.26. And see Robert Coleman, "The Dream of Cicero," *Proceedings of the Cambridge Philological Society*, n.s. 10 (1964), 1–14, who concludes that (14) "Pythagoreanism provides both the unifying theme for the whole treatise, which redeems it from the charge of being a mere scissors-and-paste composition, and also an important clue to Cicero's own political ideals. . . . So in his political writings Cicero has chosen as his chief source of inspiration a school of practising philosopher-statesmen, whose reincarnation, as he believed, had produced the finest flowering of Roman political genius."

takes as its introductory topic the verifiability of those stories that have been handed down over time. To justify his own poetic treatment of the "Marian Oak" (1.3), Cicero invokes Socrates' response to Phaedrus concerning the tale of Boreas and Orithyia (*Phaedrus* 229BC). In both his own view and Socrates', Cicero argues, fiction preserves a deeper truth by fixing continuity and change to the coordinates of time and place. Or, as Cicero so succinctly puts it to Atticus (1.3), "that is what they say" (*sic enim est traditum*)—or more literally, "so it has been handed down."

Thus the famous oak, which outlasts the flourishing of any single tree and increases in value even as its legacy is handed on, resembles not only Cicero's literary rendering in relation to past accounts but also the larger dialogue that preserves the allusion in relation to its own literary—here Platonic—inheritance. Like any other object of tradition, these cultural properties, reinvested with meaning, are simultaneously different from and the same as those embraced by previous owners as members of a society that, like any joint ownership, is in its own turn both continuous and changing.

The traditionality of literary works, in other words, follows the paradigm of *traditio* in the legal sense as the transfer of property—what Plato has called *paradosis* in the *Laws*.[31] And just as Plato's legislator of the *Laws* oversees the transfer of intellectual

31. For *traditio* in Roman law as the most widely used form of property transfer (or *alienatio*) see Buckland, 228-32; Schultz, 349-51; Thomas, 179-83; Watson, *Law of Property in the Later Roman Republic*, 61-62 and *Roman Private Law around 200 B.C.*, 65-66 esp. 65: "*Traditio* was the mode for voluntarily transferring corporeal *res nec mancipi* and it involved no formalities but only actual physical delivery of the thing. Delivery would, of course, have to be accompanied by some intention to transfer and receive ownership, and ownership would not be acquired if, for instance, the thing was handed over and received under contract of hire." See also *Gai institutiones*, II.19-20 and chapter 1, above.

as well as material property, so in *De legibus,* Cicero defends the common ownership of the philosophical tradition that informs the civil law; and he does so by enlisting the technical language of Roman property law (1.55):

> and since the Twelve Tables forbade ownership to be obtained by possession (*usus capionem*) within five feet of a boundary line, we will not allow the ancient possession (*veterem possessionem*) of the Academy to be displaced by this clever man [i.e. Zeno]; and we will serve as a board of three arbitrators to settle the boundary according to the Twelve Tables rather than assigning a single arbitrator by the Mamilian law.

Like the border around a ploughable field, Cicero argues, the intellectual wealth of the Academy is not subject to any claim of private ownership—not even by one, like Zeno, who has made good and constant use of it.[32]

In striking contrast to his treatment of material property, in fact, Cicero safeguards the commonality of intellectual property, and not only in this dialogue but in his most mature treatment of these issues in the *De officiis.* Indeed, the *De officiis* provides the fullest statement of both the inviolability of private property and its relation to the extended partnership that underlies the establishment and preservation of political community. As we have seen, the Greeks call this partnership/community *koinōnia,* while the Romans call it *societas.* In the *De officiis* in particular, Cicero, translating more literally, also calls it *communitas,* often

32. On *usucapio* as a means of property transfer defined as "the acquisition of *dominium* by possession for a certain time" see Buckland, 242–49 and in contradistinction to *traditio,* see Thomas, 157. For the Stoics on private property see Hutter, 125 and Wood, 112–13.

coupling this more literal translation of *koinōnia* with *societas* as the alternative rendering.

Addressing his son in his most influential political treatise, Cicero locates the origin of polities generally in the individual's need to protect his private property (2.21.73):[33]

> For the chief purpose in the establishment of consti-
> tutional state and municipal governments was that
> individual property rights might be secured. For, al-
> though it was by Nature's guidance that men were
> drawn together into communities, it was in the hope
> of safeguarding their possessions that they sought
> the protection of cities.

And while he makes no claim that natural law sanctions pri-
vate property, he does affirm the naturalness of the desire for it; therefore whatever is not unjustly or unnaturally acquired deserves the protection of law (1.7.21):

33. *De officiis,* trans. Walter Miller, LCL (Cambridge, Mass., 1913; rpt. 1975). See Wood, 105–19 and 130, esp. 105: "Because [Cicero] is the first major thinker to give such emphasis to the notion of private property and to make it a central component of his structure of social and political ideas, the neglect of the subject by most commentators is strange. Plato, Aristotle, and Polybius do, of course, recognize the significance of private property. Nevertheless, they do not give it Cicero's close attention, neither defining it so clearly nor assigning it such a crucial role in their thought."

See also Julia Annas, "Cicero on Stoic Moral Philosophy and Private Property," *Philosophia Togata: Essays on Philosophy and Roman Society,* eds. Miriam Griffin and Jonathan Barnes (Oxford, 1989), 151–73 and A. A. Long, "Cicero's politics in *De officiis,*" *Justice and Generosity: Studies in Hellenistic Social and Political Philosophy,* eds. André Laks and Malcolm Schofield (Cambridge, 1995), 213–40, esp. 233–40.

Erasmus edits the *De officiis* in 1501 and 1520. See Albert Rabil, Jr., "Cicero and Erasmus' Moral Philosophy," *Erasmus of Rotterdam Society Yearbook,* 8 (1988), 70–90.

There is, however, no such thing as private ownership established by nature, but property becomes private either through long occupancy (as in the case of those who long ago settled in unoccupied territory) or through conquest (as in the case of those who took it in war) or by due process of law, bargain, or purchase, or by allotment. . . . Therefore, inasmuch as in each case some of those things which by nature had been common property became the property of individuals, each one should retain possession of that which has fallen to his lot; and if anyone appropriates to himself anything beyond that, he will be violating the laws of human society (*ius humanae societatis*).

So long as it is acquired in accordance with the laws of society, in other words, private property finds its principal defender in these same laws.

Indeed, to disregard a citizen's right to his property is to disregard equity (*aequitas*) (2.22.78–79). And the inevitable consequences of such disregard is the destruction of society, here *societas et communitas* (3.5.22; cf. 1.7.20, 1.14.45):

so, if each one of us should seize upon the property (*commoda*) of his neighbors and take from each whatever he could appropriate to his own use, the bonds of human society (*societas hominum et communitas*) must inevitably be annihilated. For, without any conflict with Nature's laws, it is granted that everybody may prefer to secure for himself rather than for his neighbor what is essential for the conduct of life; but Nature's laws do forbid us to increase our means, wealth, and resources by despoiling (*spoliis*) others.

Warning the young Cicero against those vices that erode community, his father applauds, on the contrary, whatever virtues fortify it. For the single most important *officium* of all, as we learn at the end of book 1, is *communitas* (1.43.150–1.45.160): "that duty which is connected with the social obligation" (*a communitate*) (1.43.153). In the face of conflicting duties, Cicero asserts (1.45.160), "that class (*genus*) takes precedence which is demanded by the interests of human society (*societate*)." And if the most pressing duty is that of building community, that duty is best fostered by communication, through the sharing of information which comes from teaching, learning and what Cicero also calls more generally "communicating" (*communicando*) (1.16.50).

Furthermore, even if all political community, according to Cicero, takes property, and even private property, as its point of departure, such individual ownership pertains exclusively to material property. Here as in *De legibus*, in other words, intellectual property belongs to all in common.[34] Grouping it among those

34. While following Roman law in distinguishing between *res corporales* and *res incorporales* (see, e.g., *Topica* 5.27), where the latter has nothing to do with intellectual property, Cicero also follows Roman law in recognizing only the claim to private material property. On Roman legal attitudes toward intellectual property, and especially private intellectual property, see F. D. Prager, "The Early Growth and Influence of Intellectual Property," *Journal of the Patent Office Society*, 34 (1952), 106–40, esp. 108–17.

On the distinction between *res corporales* and *incorporales* see Thomas, 195–97 and 200; Watson, *The Law of Property in the Roman Republic*, 14 and Justinian, *Institutes*, trans. Peter Birks and Grant McLeod (Ithaca, 1987), I.2.1–3.

On *accessio* as a form of property transfer as it relates to writing and painting, see Thomas, 170–71; Watson, *Roman Private Law around 200 B.C.*, 66–68 and *Gai Institutiones*, II.77–79 and pp. 166–67: "It may be said, however, that the principle of accession does not properly apply to a

resources that suffer no diminution or loss through sharing, Cicero identifies this kind of property with the Pythagoreans and especially with their common sayings or *communia* (1.16.51–52):

> while everything assigned as private property by civil law shall be so held as prescribed by those same laws, everything else shall be regarded in the light indicated by the Greek proverb (*proverbio*): "Among friends all things in common" (*amicorum esse communia omnia*). Furthermore, we find the common property of all men in things of the sort defined by Ennius; and, though restricted by him to one instance (*in una re*), the principle may be applied (*transferri*) very generally:
>
> > "Who kindly sets a wand'rer on his way
> > Does e'en as if he lit another's lamp by his:

---

picture or to a manuscript of literary value, since they are new creations, differing in character from the materials in which they are embodied. It was indeed finally settled by Justinian that the property in the picture belonged to the painter, though the latter would be bound, as in similar cases, to make good the loss suffered by the previous owner of the canvas." Or as Justinian's *Institutes* says (II.1.34): "It would be ridiculous for a picture by Apelles or Parrhasius to accede to a board worth almost nothing."

On the other hand, Cicero does recognize that there is a common intellectual inheritance that includes the law and is every bit as worthy safeguarding as one's private property. See Wood, 131, who quotes *Pro Caecina* 70–75, esp. 75: "Wherefore you ought to hold fast what you have received from your forefathers—the public heritage of law—with no less care than the heritage of your private property; and that, not only because it is the law by which private property is hedged about, but because the individual only is affected if he abandons his inheritance, while the law cannot be abandoned without seriously affecting the community."

No less shines his, when he his friend's hath lit."

In this example (*una ex re*) he effectively teaches us all to bestow even upon a stranger what it costs us nothing to give. On this principle we have the following maxims (*communia*): "Deny no one the water that flows by;" "Let anyone who will take fire from our fire;" "Honest counsel give to one who is in doubt;" for such acts are useful to the recipient and cause the giver no loss.

Like the adages or maxims, here *communia,* so fundamental to Pythagorean training and epitomized by the one cited above on friendship and common ownership, all intellectual property rightly belongs to the community in the interest of common use.[35] The epitome of *communitas,* in turn, is *amicitia* or friendship, which Cicero identifies in the *De officiis* specifically with the social organization of the Pythagoreans.

For Pythagoras and his followers appreciated both that friendship depends on the coincidence between the morally right and the expedient and that this integration of the good and the useful informs the best societies (2.3.9–10). So Cicero reminds his son that, according to Pythagoras, a friend is a second self and friendship, like the best polities, makes unity from multiplicity (1.17.56). And so Cicero illustrates the reforming power of friendship with the story of a famous pair of Pythagorean friends (3.10.45):

35. See my "*Koinōnia* and the Friendship between Rhetoric and Religion."

On the continuity of these arguments, even on the same grounds that this property is not depleted by being shared, see Paul Goldstein, *Copyright's Highway: The Law and Lore of Copyright from Gutenberg to the Celestial Jukebox* (New York, 1994), 16–17.

They say that Damon and Phintias, of the Pythagorean school, enjoyed such ideally perfect friendship, that when the tyrant Dionysius had appointed a day for the execution of one of them, and, the one who had been condemned to death requested a few days respite for the purpose of putting his loved ones in the care of friends, the other became surety for his appearance, with the understanding that if his friend did not return, he himself should be put to death. And when the friend returned on the appointed day, the tyrant in admiration for their faithfulness (*fides*) begged that they would enrol him as a third partner in their friendship.

In striking contrast to the friend as the epitome of the just man, the tyrant, as we have seen, uses all of the commonwealth as his own private property; and yet even the tyrant admires the *fides* of such friendship, aspiring to belong to such a partnership.[36] Indeed, *fides* or trust is the basis not only of *amicitia* but also of *iustitia* or justice, the basis in turn of any commonwealth (1.7.23). Considering *amicitia* absolutely central to any treatment of politics, Cicero sends his readers, including his son, to his fuller treatment of the subject in the *De amicitia* (2.9.31).

Written shortly before the *De officiis*, this dialogue on friendship embraces both the Pythagorean adages about friendship and, rejecting the materialism of the so-called moderns, the ancient teachings about the soul and its journeys. Indeed, the principal speaker, Laelius, echoes Scipio in assigning the antimaterialism already traditional in Plato jointly to Pythagoras and to Socrates; only here Laelius adds the further corroboration of the ancient Romans, who, like these Greek philosophers, attended

36. See Konstan, 114–15 and Wood, 136.

equally to the migrations of the soul (4.13). In fact, Laelius reminds his listeners in the *De amicitia* of Scipio's own views on this matter as recorded in *De re publica* (4.14):[37]

> [Scipio], as if with a premonition of his fate, discoursed for three days on the commonwealth, and devoted almost all of the conclusion of his discussion to the immortality of the soul, making use of arguments which he had heard, he said, from Africanus the Elder through a vision in his sleep. If the truth really is that the souls of all good men after death make the easiest escape from what may be termed the imprisonment and fetters of the flesh, whom can we think of as having had an easier journey to the gods than Scipio? Therefore, I fear that grief at such a fate as his would be a sign more of envy than of friendship.

Recalling the events of the *De re publica*, Laelius' account of the *somnium Scipionis* rehearses a tradition of political theory that regularly situates its discussions of the commonwealth in a broader landscape of topics that include friendship and psychic migration. As we have seen, all three doctrines characterize Pythagoreanism and find their fullest early expression in Plato's *Republic*.

Like Plato's *Laws* and Aristotle's *Politics*, however, Cicero's

37. Cicero, *De amicitia*, trans. William Armistead Falconer, LCL (Cambridge, Mass., 1923; rpt. 1996). And see P. A. Brunt, "'Amicitia' in the Later Roman Republic," *Proceedings of the Cambridge Philological Society*, n.s. 11 (1965), 1–20; Hutter, 133–74; David Konstan, "Friendship and the State: The Context of Cicero's *De amicitia*," *Hyperboreus*, 2 (1994/5), 1–16 and *Friendship in the Classical World*, 122–33; and J. E. G. Zetzel, "Cicero and the Scipionic Circle," *Harvard Studies in Classical Philology*, 76 (1972), 173–79.

political theory withdraws from the communalism of Croton, at least on the issue of material property. In contrast to the Pythagoreans, the friends of the *De amicitia* hold *almost* all things in common. As Cicero has Laelius remember in regard to his friendship with Scipio—a friendship that sets the standard for Cicero's own intimacy with Atticus (1.5)—they lived, ate, worked, studied and talked together (4.15, 27.103-04). Being of one mind, however, Cicero's idealized friends were not of one purse. Like Roman law, Roman friendship makes division between ownership of intellectual and material property—a division that cenobitic monasticism, returning to the Pythagorean communalism of Croton, will once again erase.

5

Pythagoreans and Christians on Traditioning the Common Life

While mining the texts of the ancient philosophers for their proverbial riches, Erasmus discovers in these same texts just how central a role property played in ancient political theory. At the same time, he also discovers the commonalities between the political philosophy traditionally associated with Pythagoras and his followers (including Plato) and the earliest forms of cenobitic monasticism. These commonalities must in turn have reinforced Erasmus' commitment to *philosophia Christi;* for they speak most eloquently to just those traditions shared by the ancients and early Christians.[1] Not surprisingly, these commonalities also find their way back into his treatment of more than a few adages. Indeed, the opening adage on friendship and common property not only cites the very same works examined in the previous chapter—Plato's *Republic* and *Laws,* Aristotle's *Politics,* Cicero's *De legibus* and *De officiis*—but ends with the authority of Pythagoras, and more precisely, as we will soon see in more detail, with an endorsement of Pythagorean cenobitism as forerunner of the most exalted Christian way of life.

In a later, equally well-known adage (II.v.1), "Spartam nactus es, hanc orna" ("Sparta is your portion; do your best for her"), Erasmus rehearses the opening adage's philosophy of common

---

1. For the late antique notion of *philosophia Christi* see J. Leclercq, "Pour l'histoire de l'expression 'philosophie chrétienne,'" *Mélanges de Science Religieuse,* 9 (1952), 221–26 and *The Love of Learning and the Desire for God,* trans. Catharine Misrahi (New York, 1982), 100–01.

ownership. On this particular occasion, however, he invokes the Pythagorean proverb as part of his case against the contemporary political practice of waging war in the interests of acquiring foreign property (LB, II, 552F–553A, *CWE*, 33, 239):

> If every prince were to try to improve what he has been given, we may be sure all things would flourish universally; and among friends of course, who are Christians, all things will be common to all. As things are, it often happens that we try to undermine the possessions of others, and entirely overthrow our own.

Recalling both the political context and the moral lesson of the adage "The half is more than the whole," discussed in chapter 1, Erasmus here warns the good Christian prince to attend to the needs of his citizens. Instead of depleting their material resources in the cause of territorial expansion, he should rather strive to leave the commonwealth he has inherited better off than he found it. So apt is this proverbial wisdom to political life that Erasmus offers it again in his manual for princes, the *Institutio principis christiani*, reintroducing the same adage as a slogan appropriate for all rulers (*ASD* IV-I, 212; *CWE*, 27, 281):[2]

> Not without reason have Theopompus' words been much praised; he said that he was not interested in how large a kingdom he left to his sons, only in how much better and secure it was. It seems to me that that Laconic proverb "You have drawn Sparta, now enhance it" (*Spartam sortitus es, hanc orna*) might be inscribed on the arms of every prince.

2. See James D. Tracy, *The Politics of Erasmus: A Pacifist Intellectual and His Political Milieu* (Toronto, 1978), 59–66.

110 / Pythagoreans and Christians on Traditioning the Common Life

Adapting, as Erasmus himself points out, an aphoristic method not unlike that of proverbial statement, the *Institutio* holds much in common with this adage.[3] Both appreciate the fundamental role of property in political philosophy; and both look back to the philosophers of Greek and Roman antiquity, especially Plato, for the source of their appreciation.

Like Plato and his ancient followers, as we have seen in the previous chapter, Erasmus distinguishes between the king and the tyrant according to how they view their subjects' property. For the tyrant treats not only his subjects' goods but his subjects themselves as his own property, whereas the good ruler holds himself responsible for protecting the goods of those he rules. In other—more aphoristic—words, "he who looks to the common good is a king; he who looks to his own good is a tyrant" (*ASD* IV-I, 174; *CWE*, 27, 244). In the end, however, both king and tyrant own everything. For the citizens of a commonwealth justly ruled, Erasmus contends, willingly put their possessions and even their lives at the king's disposal when necessary (*ASD* IV-I, 160; *CWE*, 27, 229). In this way, the king, unlike the tyrant, rightly considers his own everything his subjects possess.

Further in keeping with Plato's political theory, Erasmus also argues for the closest alignment between politics and philosophy. Only the prince who is also a philosopher can avoid the decline into tyranny (*ASD* IV-I, 144; *CWE*, 27, 214). By philosopher, however, Erasmus has something other than the usual profile in mind (*ASD* IV-I, 144–45; *CWE*, 27, 214):

3. Ep. 393, Allen, II, 207, *CWE*, 27, 204: "I have taken Isocrates' work on the principles of government and translated it into Latin, and in competition with him I have added my own, arranged as it were in aphorisms for the reader's convenience, but with considerable differences from what he laid down." On the usefulness of adages in the prince's education, see *ASD* IV-I, 140; *CWE*, 27, 210.

Further, you must realize that "philosopher" does not mean someone who is clever at dialectics or science but someone who rejects illusory appearance and undauntedly seeks out and follows what is true and good. Being a philosopher is in practice the same as being a Christian; only the terminology is different.

For the advocate of *philosophia Christi*, in other words, philosophy itself—at least the right kind of philosophy, including political philosophy—shares much in common with Christianity, at least the right kind of Christianity. In the well-known letter that introduces the *Enchiridion*, Erasmus encourages his friend Paul Volz to reflect on precisely this commonality. Erasmus also invites him in this same letter to think about the right kind of monasticism. For in their earliest formation, Erasmus insists on the one hand, monastic communities were nothing other than associations of friends willingly practicing together the kind of life featured in the New Testament (Ep. 858, Allen, III, 375; *CWE*, 66, 21). And on the other, he asks in this same prefatory letter, what else is a city but a vast monastery (Allen, III, 376; *CWE*, 66, 22)?[4]

Embracing some key principles of Plato's political theory, then, Erasmus discerns these same principles in the earliest Christian monastic movements, and not least of all in relation to issues of property. In keeping with this understanding, Erasmus concludes the 1515 and all subsequent editions of our first adage on friendship and common property by identifying cenobitic monasticism with the same Pythagorean *koinōnia* that, as

4. Cf. *De opere monachorum* in *Oeuvres de Saint Augustin,* ed. J. Saint-Martin (Paris, 1949), III, 25.33: "Omnium enim Christianorum una respublica est."

I have argued in the previous chapter, informs the organization of Plato's ideal city (LB, II, 14EF, *CWE*, 31, 30):

> For all those who were admitted by Pythagoras into that well-known band who followed his instruction would give to the common fund whatever money and family property they possessed. This is called in Latin, in a word which expresses the facts, *coeno-bium*, clearly from community (*societate*) of life and fortunes.

In this particular case, however, Erasmus' authority is not Plato but Aulus Gellius, or so Erasmus believes. For in the essay of the *Attic Nights* on Pythagorean training, *disciplina pythagorica* (1.9), where Erasmus thinks he has discovered the shared practice of cenobitism, Aulus Gellius has actually written not *koinobion*, as mistakenly published in the earliest editions of his *Noctes Atticae*, but *ercto non cito*, an unfamiliar Roman legal formula.[5]

And yet, in spite of this misreading, it is worth noting, Erasmus draws a conclusion that is philosophically, even if not philologically, sound. For the second-century Roman lawyer, like the sixteenth-century theologian, is taking special notice of the ancient Italian philosopher's position on property. Regarding the Pythagorean initiates at Croton, Aulus Gellius records that "as

---

5. Aulus Gellius, *The Attic Nights,* trans. John C. Rolfe, LCL (Cambridge, Mass., 1927; rpt. 1984), 3 vols. See also *A. Gellii Noctes Atticae,* ed. P. K. Marshall (Oxford, 1968), 2 vols.

On the legal formula *ercto non cito* see *De oratore,* 1.56.237 and Servius, *Comm. Aen.* VIII, 642. And see Alan Watson, *The Law of Property in the Later Roman Republic* (Oxford, 1968), 110, 121–24 and *Roman Private Law around 200 B.C.* (Edinburgh, 1971), 140–43. See also Edwin L. Minar, Jr., "Pythagorean Communism," *TAPA,* 75 (1944), 34–46 and David Wootton, "Friendship Portrayed: A New Account of *Utopia,*" 36–37.

soon as they had been admitted by Pythagoras into that band of disciples, [they] at once devoted to the common use whatever estate and property they had, and an inseparable fellowship (*societas inseparabilis*) was formed, like the old-time association which in Roman legal parlance was termed an 'undivided inheritance' (*ercto non cito*)" (1.9.12). Like the late antique biographical essay, then, the Erasmian adage draws attention to this remarkable custom, striking to both the antique Roman and the sixteenth-century European, of holding property in common. Whereas the Roman lawyer compares Pythagorean communalism to a special legal disposition of an inherited estate, the Dutch theologian associates it with the religious common life.

While it may be the most striking Pythagorean practice recorded by Aulus Gellius, common ownership of material property is not the only practice of significance to an advocate of Christian philosophy. Alongside an education focused on some of the subjects of the liberal arts, including music, geometry, and astronomy (cf. *De vita Pythagorica* 158), Pythagorean training or discipline, as outlined in this essay, also features two kinds of exercises: keeping silent (*echemuthia*) (1.9.5; cf. *De vita pythagorica* 94 and *Adages*, III.x.1) and meditating on the texts studied — what Aulus Gellius here refers to as *meditari* (1.9.6). As we have seen in chapter three, Plato calls this practice of meditation *meletē*, from the Greek verb *meletan*. As we have also seen, *meletē* forms part of the *askēsis* fundamental to the philosophical life.[6]

6. On the roles of *meletē* and *askēsis* in ancient philosophy see Pierre Hadot, *Philosophy as a Way of Life*, 49–89 and 112, n. 38, quoted above. On the "prehistory of these exercises in Pythagoreanism" see 116, n. 79. See also Mary Carruthers, *The Craft of Thought*, 80–81, 105–12 and Jean Leclercq, *Etudes sur le vocabulaire monastique du moyen age* (Rome, 1961), 134–38.

For Aulus Gellius, so the heading of his essay reveals, *disciplina* not only corresponds to but actually translates Platonic *askesis*.[7]

The essay from the *Attic Nights* characterizing the philosophical life as lived by the Pythagorean is one important source informing Erasmus' understanding of the common inheritance of ancient philosophy and so-called Christian philosophy. Two others of equal importance are Diogenes Laertius' life of Pythagoras from his collection entitled *Lives and Opinions of Eminent Philosophers* (book 8) and Iamblichus' *On the Pythagorean Life*. Not incidentally, Diogenes Laertius' Pythagoras is a philosopher of both friendship and education; he is also a political theorist and even a political reformer (8.6). Paving the way for Plato and Aristotle, this Pythagoras appreciates not only the role of education in political life but also the pedagogical value of performing the duties of citizenship in a well-governed community (8.16). The members of Pythagoras' community, according to his biographer, participate in ritual washings (8.33), communal singing of hymns (8.24), and a memory discipline or *askēsis* that concentrates the mind (8.23; cf. *De vita pythagorica*, 165, 256). The portrait of Pythagoras detailed in this biography, moreover, corresponds to that of Iamblichus in his much longer essay on the Pythagorean way of life.

The Pythagoras of the *De vita pythagorica* is also a man deeply committed to both politics and education as constitutive of the philosophical life.[8] Recalling the political philosophy of Plato

7. See Hadot, *Philosophy as a Way of Life*, 82, 128; Anthony Meredith, "Asceticism—Christian and Greek," *Journal of Theological Studies*, N.S. 27 (1976), 313-32 and R. A. Markus, *The End of Ancient Christianity* (Cambridge, 1990), 73-74.

8. On Iamblichus' intense interest in education, in contrast to Porphyry, who also writes a life of Pythagoras, and on the place of Pythagoras

and Aristotle discussed in the previous chapter, Pythagorean political community or *koinōnia* takes justice or *dikē* as the essential relation between its members and friendship or *philia* as the finest social expression of that relation. So Iamblichus reminds his readers that Pythagoras finds the best form of *politeia* reflected in the adage that friends hold all things in common (32; cf. 72, 81, 92, 168, 235). And so he locates commonality, with equality, as the source of justice, charting in the process the genealogy of the Platonic ideal (167):

> The origin of justice, then, is community feeling and fairness (*to koinon kai ison*), for all to share experience, approximating as closely as possible to one body and one soul, and for everyone to say "mine" and "someone else's" about the same thing (just as Plato also testifies, having learnt it from the Pythagoreans).

Before Plato, according to Iamblichus, Pythagoras contrasted the fairness of sharing with the unfairness of taking more than one's share or *pleonexia* (68, 77–78, 168, 225); and before Plato, he characterized the tyrant as not only unjust but also unfriended (189). Those who govern justly, by contrast, function as trustees of the *politeia*, holding themselves responsible to its citizens for returning the commonwealth to them no less prosperous than it was handed over (46).

---

and Plato in this *paideia*, see Bent Dalsgaard Larsen, *Iamblique de Chalcis: exégète et philosophe* (Aarhus, 1972), 80–100 and *Iamblichi Chalcidensis in Platonis Dialogos: Commentariorum Fragmenta*, ed. and trans. John M. Dillon (Leiden, 1973), 11–15. On the different status of poetry in the *paideia* of Pythagoras and that of Plato, see C. J. De Vogel, 80 and cf. *De vita pythagorica* 110.

On this first book of the whole corpus see Dominic O'Meara, *Pythagoras Revived* (Oxford, 1989), 30–85.

An advocate of political communalism, including common ownership of material property, Iamblichus' Pythagoras is also an advocate of sharing intellectual property. Indeed, education or *paideia* is nothing other than the collective genius or *koinē euphuïa* of the best minds passed on to others (43).[9] Unlike material property, however, intellectual wealth can be given to others without loss to the giver (43). In this way, education functions within political community to distribute that property which is most readily shared. Pythagoras' first students, Iamblichus tells us, came to Samos expressly to have a share (*koinōnein*) in the education he provided (28). And Iamblichus draws attention not only to Pythagoras' willingness to communicate this intellectual property but also to the peculiar form his communications take. For Pythagoras hands over both the wisdom of the ancient Egyptians and their method for traditioning this wisdom (103–05; cf. 20, 145):

> But the most necessary form of teaching, for Pythagoras, was by symbols. Almost all Greeks were enthusiastic about this kind of teaching, because it is of very great antiquity: the Egyptians gave it its most subtle (*poikilōtata*) form and highest status. In the same way Pythagoras also valued it greatly, as may be seen by those who can perceive the meaning and unspoken content of the Pythagorean symbols (*Pythagorikōn symbolōn*), and can realise how much rightness and truth is in them once they are freed from the concealment of their riddling form, and how well their simple and straightforward transmission (*haplēn kai apoikilon paradosin*) suits the greatness, indeed the closeness to god which surpasses

9. See C. J. De Vogel, 96 and Larsen, 98.

human understanding, of these philosophers. . . . Unless one can interpret the symbols, and understand them by careful exposition (*exēgēsei*), what they say would strike the chance observer as absurd — old wives' tales, full of nonsense and idle talk. But once they are deciphered as symbols should be, and become clear and transparent instead of obscure to outsiders, they impress us like utterances of the gods or Delphic oracles, revealing an astounding intellect and having a supernatural influence on those lovers of learning (*philologōn*) who have understood them.

As we have already seen, at least one humanist *philologos* did appreciate the "ocean of philosophy" (as he put it) contained in these seemingly absurd and trivial sayings (see above, and cf. *De vita pythagorica* 162). Advertising the silenus-like nature of proverbs, as we will see in more detail later in this chapter, this same philologist also opened his collection of proverbs with the very same *pythagorae symbola* that Iamblichus here extols, noting, as we have already seen, that whole Platonic dialogues are comprehensible as amplifications of these tiny sayings (LB, II, 7AB; *CWE*, 31, 15).

Erasmus' claim concerning Plato's rhetorical practice, moreover, reverses the hermeneutical practice that becomes the hallmark of Iamblichus' educational program. For Iamblichus not only sets the reading list for his students, including the order in which the prescribed Platonic dialogues should be read, but he also teaches them how to read these works, encouraging them to begin their exegeses by finding what he calls the *skopos*. Like the Pythagorean proverb or *symbolon* in unifying complex and variegated expressions of wisdom into a single statement, the *skopos* of a literary text articulates its thematic unity in a single, brief formulation that through interpretation explains in turn the manifold variety of that text. Once the reader identifies the *skopos*, which all parts of the text hold in common insofar as they belong to a unified whole, she can then go on to interpret the details in light of their commonality. Not surprisingly, Iamblichus takes his mandate for reading this way from Plato himself, and especially from Socrates' observations in the *Phaedrus* concerning the organic nature of skillfully crafted discourse, defined as discourse in which one part relates not only to all the other parts but to the whole (*Phaedrus* 264C).[10]

This relation of parts to whole is fundamental to Iamblichus' hermeneutics. And while the *De vita pythagorica* does not directly address the principles and practices of interpretation taught in his school, it does lay bare the epistemological presupposition behind his methods—not on the authority of Pythagoras himself, however, but on that of one of his earliest disciples (160):[11]

> knowledge of the part follows from knowledge of the whole. "People who have an exact knowledge of the whole," says Archytas, "will see the parts correctly, as they are." That is why the things which exist are not isolated, unique, simple (*hapla*), but are seen as complex (*poikila*) and varied.

10. On the hermeneutical uses of *skopos*, including its justification in a reading of the *Phaedrus*, see Dillon, 56, 92–99 and Larsen, 432–53. On its rhetorical, and especially Ciceronian origins, see Larsen, 437. On the continuing role of *skopos* in hermeneutics see Carruthers, *The Craft of Thought*, 79–82; Eden, *Hermeneutics and the Rhetorical Tradition*, 84, 98–100 and Georges Florovsky, "The Function of Tradition in the Ancient Church," *Greek Orthodox Theological Review*, 9 (1963/64), 188–91. On the complementarity more generally between literary composition and reception—rhetoric and hermeneutics—see my *Hermeneutics and the Rhetorical Tradition*.

11. On Archytas see Diogenes Laertius, 8.79–83.

Iamblichus presupposes, in other words, that the whole, characterized by uniformity and simplicity—*to haploos*—is prior to the complexity and variegation or *poikilia* of the parts; and this priority obtains both in cognition and in interpretation. Where the texts being interpreted are *symbola*, moreover, Iamblichus further assumes two important discrepancies: one is between the apparent absurdity of a form of expression that is *poikilōtata*—that is, so complicated as to be enigmatic—and the clarity and profundity of its wisdom (cf. 157); the other is between this same *poikilia* of statement and the simplicity or straightforwardness (*to haploos*) of its transmission or *paradosis*.[12]

Indeed, throughout the *De vita pythagorica*, Iamblichus pays special attention to the traditioning or handing down not only of these *symbola* but of all the practices and principles of the philosophical life as lived by Pythagoreans. Among the practices traditioned Iamblichus includes those of friendship (229), courageous action (ch. 32) and the wearing of white linen (149), and among the principles, those concerning harmony (121) and legislation (ch. 27).

Iamblichus is most attentive to the traditioning of the *pythagorae symbola*, however, because of their role in education. For they are "preparation for philosophy . . . handed down (*paredothē*) as education (*paideian*) only to those who know, in accordance with the practice of the Egyptians and the most ancient Greek theologians" (ch. 23; Clark, p. 45). In chapter 29 he then returns to these same symbols that convey "the knowledge (*tēn epistēmēn*) [Pythagoras] handed down (*paradidosin*) from the beginning about the objects of thought and about the gods" (157). Famous for his commitment to the common distribution

12. On the opposition in ancient philosophy, especially Platonism, between *to haploos* and *to poikilon* see Wesley Trimpi, *Muses of One Mind*, 133–43, 235–40 and Eden, *Hermeneutics and the Rhetorical Tradition*, 35.

of material property, Pythagoras, according to Iamblichus, is no less committed to the passing on or traditioning of this common intellectual property (158, 161, 166, 229). Among the things that friends in the Pythagorean sense hold in common, then, are these commonest of sayings (cf. Diogenes Laertius, 8.16) and the education or *paideia* of which they are a part.

As argued previously, living the philosophical life Pythagorean-style depends on a particular *paideia* or education. It also depends on a special training or *askēsis*.[13] So Iamblichus includes in his description of this life intelligence-training (42), memory-training (164), training in the rituals of purification (ch. 16), and training in acting moderately (131) and courageously (ch. 32). Like Pythagorean *paideia*, moreover, Pythagorean *askēsis* requires a carefully guarded tradition or *paradosis*. So Iamblichus begins chapter 20 by introducing his readers to (p. 42) "The special practices (*askēmata*) of Pythagorean philosophy; how he handed them down (*paredidou*) and how he exercised each new generation embarking on philosophy." And so he supplements his treatment of a branch of education supposedly invented by Pythagoras—namely political education or *paideia politikē* (130–31)—with a discussion of both an *askēsis* and *paradosis* of its single most important virtue (186; cf. *Adages*, I.i.2):

> His saying "Do not step over the yoke" is an exhortation to justice and an instruction to practice (*askein*) all just actions, as will be shown in my dis-

13. On the daily routine or *epitēdeumata* of the Pythagoreans, see ch. 21 and 96–100. This routine includes both solitary and communal walks, study, physical exercise, collaboration on administrative and legal problems, communal meals, readings and singing of hymns to the gods. On its relation to early monastic routine, see De Vogel, 186–87; Larsen, 84 and Markus, *The End of Ancient Christianity*, 73–78. On Pythagorean *askēsis* see Meredith, 313–32 and Larsen, 84.

cussion of symbols (*symbolōn*). So through all these
Pythagoras manifested great concern for training
(*askein*) in justice, and established a tradition (*paradosin*) of justice in words and deeds alike.

Even before Plato, in other words, Pythagoras (according to
Iamblichus) conceives of the philosophical life as profoundly
political—a *koinōnia* in the strictest sense, where all things are
held in common.[14] For this commonality and equality are the
basis of justice. Also before Plato, Pythagoras (according to
Iamblichus) insisted that those living this kind of life require not
only commonly held principles but also commonly held practices: an *askēsis* as well as a *paideia*. The continuity of this community over time requires in turn a way of passing both teaching and training on from one generation to the next; it requires
tradition or *paradosis*.

An astute reader of these late antique biographies, as the
Adages attests, Erasmus could hardly have overlooked the commonalities between the philosophical life as described by Aulus Gellius, Diogenes Laertius, and Iamblichus, and the earliest
Christian communities as described by such advocates of cenobitism as Basil of Caesarea and Augustine of Hippo, with whose
works Erasmus had an editor's familiarity.[15] In the writings of
Basil, for instance, and especially in his various discussions of

14. On Pythagoras' influence on Platonic political theory, Iamblichus
claims (131): "If we calculate the angles at which the lines meet, and the
squares on each side, we have an excellent model of a constitution (*politeia*). Plato appropriated this idea, when he expressly mentioned, in the
Republic, the first two numbers in the ratio of four to three which join
with the fifth to make the two harmonies." See also 179 and Larsen, 98.

On Pythagorean politics see Kurt von Fritz, *Pythagorean Politics in
Southern Italy: An Analysis of the Sources* (New York, 1940).

15. For Erasmus' edition of Augustine see ch. 1, above, n. 9. His edition
of Basil appeared in 1532.

monastic life, Erasmus would find the same emphasis not only on *koinōnia* but also on its related elements of *askēsis, meletē,* and *paradosis.*

So the sixth and seventh rules of the *Longer Rules* of Basil's so-called *Asceticon* (362–65 C.E.) call for withdrawal from the kind of *koinos bios* that prevents meditation or *meletē* into the kind of common life that fosters it (344BC). In this right kind of *koinōnia,* like-minded friends in God share all things in common (346DE), including not only their material property but also their intellectual gifts (346E):[16]

> So that of necessity in the community life (*tōi koinō-nikōi biōi*) the working of the Holy Spirit in one man passes over to all the rest at once. Now all you who have read the Gospels know the great danger incurred by the man living alone, who has one gift perhaps, and makes it useless by idleness, digging a hole for it in himself. Whereas when a number live together a man enjoys his own gift, multiplying it by imparting it to others, and reaps the fruits of other men's gifts as if they were his own.

While taking the apostolic community of Acts as its model, Basilian *koinōnia,* as students of early Christianity regularly note, inherits many of its features from the philosophical life of Greco-Roman antiquity.[17] Basil's concern with *koinobion* in the

16. *The Ascetic Works of Saint Basil,* trans. W. K. L. Clarke (London, 1925), 164–65; PG 31, 932. See George L. Kustas, "Saint Basil and the Rhetorical Tradition," *Basil of Caesarea: Christian, Humanist, Ascetic,* ed. Paul J. Fedwick (Toronto, 1981), 225–26.

17. On the Platonic elements in the apostolic community of Acts see David L. Mealand, "Community of Goods and Utopian Allusions in Acts II–IV," *Journal of Theological Studies,* N.S. 28 (1977), 96–99. See also Alan C. Mitchell, "The Social Function of Friendship in Acts 2:44–47

Longer Rules, moreover, corresponds with his characterization of it in a letter to his friend Gregory Nazianzus.

In this letter (Ep. 2), as in the *Rules,* Basil advises the Christian to withdraw from the world (*kosmou de anachōrēsis*) — a withdrawal or *anachōrēsis* more psychological than physical (I, 11).[18] By doing so, the anchorite better achieves the aim of retirement: *askēsis* or discipline (Ep. 2, I, 13). An important element of this discipline, along with praying and singing, is *meletē* or studying Scripture (I, 15):[19]

---

and 4:32–37," *Journal of Biblical Literature,* 111 (1992), 255–72. For Basil's adaptation of the ancient philosophical life see Philip Rousseau, *Basil of Caesarea* (Berkeley, 1994), 61–92. And see Jean Leclercq, *Etudes sur le vocabulaire monastique du moyen age,* 39–48.

On Basilian monasticism see David Amand, *L'Ascèse Monastique de Saint Basile* (Maredsous, 1949), esp. 118–28; Clarke, 11–45; Markus, *The End of Ancient Christianity,* 73–75, 158. On the relation between this monasticism and the antique philosophical life, see Hadot, 107 and 140: "Generally speaking, we can say that monasticism in Egypt and Syria was born and developed in a Christian milieu, spontaneously and without the intervention of a philosophical model. . . . Under Alexandrian influence however—the distant influence of Philo, and the more immediate influence of Origen and Clement of Alexandria, magnificently orchestrated by the Cappadocians—certain philosophical spiritual techniques were introduced into Christian spirituality. The result of this was that the Christian ideal was described, and, in part, practiced, by borrowing models and vocabulary from the Greek philosophical tradition. Thanks to its literary and philosophical qualities, this tendency became dominant, and it was through its agency that the heritage of ancient spiritual exercises was transmitted to Christian spirituality."

For Basil's familiarity with Platonism and Pythagoreanism, including the influence of Iamblichus, see John M. Rist, "Basil's 'Neoplatonism': Its Background and Nature," *Basil of Caesarea: Christian, Humanist, Ascetic,* 137–220 and Amand, 61–72. On Basilian *koinōnia* in both rhetorical and religious contexts see Kustas, 221–79.

18. *The Letters,* trans. Roy J. Deferrari (London, 1926), 4 vols. For the Platonism of this letter see Rist, "Basil's 'Neoplatonism,'" 213.

19. For the Platonism of Basilian *askēsis,* see Rousseau, 79–81; and on

A most important path to the discovery of duty
is also the study (*meletē*) of the divinely-inspired
Scriptures. For in them are not only found the precepts of conduct, but also the lives of saintly men,
recorded and handed down (*paradedomenoi*) to us,
lie before us like living images (*eikones empsychoi*) of
God's government (*tēs kata theon politeias*), for our
imitation of their good works.

Not unlike reading Plato's *Republic* or *Laws,* in other words,
studying Scripture, according to Basil, provides precepts and examples for communal life. A work of (among other things) *politeia,* Scripture is traditioned to all Christians so that they might
put its program into practice in their own communities.

Basil's commitment to both the common life and to the role of
Scripture in traditioning this life is further confirmed by his fullest discussion of tradition itself. In the *De Spiritu Sancto* (c. 374
C.E.) Basil argues vigorously against the subordination of the
Holy Spirit on the basis of *paradosis* or tradition, and especially
on the basis of what has been traditioned concerning the relation
between Father and Son (7:16):[20]

---

his ascetic writings more generally, 190–232. On *meditatio,* see Rousseau,
223–24. See also John Dillon, *The Middle Platonists,* 341–83 and Jaroslav
Pelikan, *Christianity and Classical Culture: The Metamorphosis of Natural
Theology in the Christian Encounter with Hellenism* (New Haven, 1993).
On *anachōrēsis* or withdrawal see A.-J. Festugière, *Personal Religion among
the Greeks* (Berkeley, 1954), esp. 53–67.

According to Heninger, *Touches of Sweet Harmony,* 66 n. 49, the Aldine
Epistolae Basilii Magni et al. (1499) contained three letters attributed to
Pythagoras' wife.

20. *The Treatise De Spiritu Sancto,* trans. Blomfield Jackson in *Nicene
and Post-Nicene Fathers,* eds. Philip Schaff and Henry Wace (New York,
1895), VIII, 10.

For Basil's understanding of tradition not only in legal terms but, more

What our fathers said, the same say we, that the glory of the Father and of the Son is common (*koinē*); wherefore we offer the doxology to the Father *with* the Son. But we do not rest only on the fact that such is the tradition of the Fathers; for they too followed the sense of Scripture, and started from the evidence which, a few sentences back, I deduced from Scripture and laid before you.

Deriving from Scripture itself, Basil claims, the *koinōnia* between Father and Son extends to include the Holy Spirit. Indeed, among the three there is an "inseparable fellowship" reminiscent of Aulus Gellius' *societas inseparabilis* characterizing Pythagorean community. So Basil concludes, in regard to the three co-equal partners of the Trinity (26.63), "whenever the fellowship (*koinōnia*) is intimate, congenital and inseparable, the word *with* is more expressive, suggesting, as it does, the idea of inseparable fellowship (*achōristos koinōnia*)."

For Basil, then, *koinōnia* understood in the Pythagorean sense of holding all things in common characterizes the best form of

---

precisely, like equity, as the intention or meaning of Scripture in contrast to the words themselves, see Florovsky, "The Function of Tradition in the Ancient Church," 193–97; Tad W. Guzie, "Patristic Hermeneutics and the Meaning of Tradition," *Theological Studies*, 32 (1971), 647–58; R. P. C. Hanson, "Basil's Doctrine of Tradition in Relation to the Holy Spirit," *Vigiliae Christianae*, 22 (1968), 241–55 and Rousseau, 117–29. And see Ep. 160, Deferrari, II, 403–07. For a similar position among other early Church Fathers see Outler, 8–30 and Johannes Quasten, "Tertullian and 'Traditio,'" *Traditio*, 2 (1944), 481–84. On the association of the equitable reading of both *scriptum* and *scriptura* with the intention in contrast to the words of the text see my *Hermeneutics and the Rhetorical Tradition*.

On the *koinōnia* between the three persons of the Trinity see Kustas, 232–33.

Christian *politeia* as epitomized in monastic living.[21] It also characterizes the relation between the three persons of the Trinity. For both characterizations, Basil seeks authorization in apostolic tradition, itself understood as the *paideia* handed down from Jesus to his earliest disciples. For just as the apostles followed Jesus' command in sharing among themselves material property, so, Basil insists, they traditioned his truths to be shared among all believers. Like their other possessions, this possession too must be held in common.

Like Basil (and maybe even to some extent following him), Augustine vigorously defends both common ownership of material property as the basis of monastic living and the commonality of the divinely revealed truths of Scripture.[22] So the Augustinian *Regula* insists on community property, *omnia communia:* "Do not call anything your own; possess everything in common" (1.3);[23] and so Augustine structures *communitas* around both co-

21. See Markus, 158 and Hadot, 140. See also Kustas, 253, on the role of *oikeiotēs* not only in Basil's monasticism but also in his understanding of the relation of classical to Christian culture: "For some Neoplatonists οἰκειότης becomes almost an obsession: it helped describe for them the transcendent unity after which they sought. . . . under its aegis individual and society can effectively interact, as in a monastic community, and in the clash between Christianity and classical culture it could signal the way to cooperation." On *oikeiotēs* in Basil's *Ad adolescentes,* see my *Hermeneutics and the Rhetorical Tradition,* 42–53.

22. For the influence of Basilian on Augustinian *coenobium* see George Lawless, *Augustine of Hippo and his Monastic Rule* (Oxford, 1987), xi, 42–52 and Markus, *The End of Ancient Christianity,* 158–63.

23. Lawless, *Augustine of Hippo and his Monastic Rule,* 81. Concerning the sources for Augustine's *Rule,* Lawless makes a claim central to the argument of this book (124): "There frankly was no need for them to acknowledge derivative material. Writings of fellow Christians were in those days regarded as common property, a patrimony which could

operative labor and, recalling the Pythagorean routine outlined by Iamblichus, the more leisurely "group activities" of walking, dining, talking, praying, reading, and singing hymns. Life in the *monasterium,* in other words, resembles in many important details communal life for the first Pythagorean initiates at Croton. Like Pythagorean friends, Augustine's "friends in God" hold all things in common.[24]

Indeed, friendship or *amicitia,* underlying the practices as well as the principles of Augustine's social philosophy, provides the conceptual framework for his actual attempts at monastic living, including the failed experiment at Rome, the withdrawal to Cassiciacum and eventually the monastery at Thagaste. From

---

be handily appropriated by a later Christian writer in the interests of edification."

See also Charles W. Brockwell, "Augustine's Ideal of Monastic Community: A Paradigm for his Doctrine of the Church," *Augustinian Studies,* 8 (1977), 91–107 and Andrea Gerlin, "Community and Ascesis: Paul's Directives to the Corinthians Integrated in the Rule of Augustine," *Collectanea Augustiniana,* eds. Joseph C. Schnaubelt and Frederick van Fleteren (New York, 1990), 303–13.

24. On the similarities between the Pythagorean and Augustinian routines, see Markus, 77–78; R. J. Halliburton, "The Inclination to Retirement—the Retreat of Cassiciacum and the 'Monastery' of Thagaste," *Studia Patristica,* 5 (1962), 329–40 and especially Lawless, 40 and 33, where his remark on this issue is to the point (33): "Pedagogically, therefore, the composition of both the dialogue *On order* and Augustine's *Rule* are strikingly similar. Pythagorean and monastic precepts are directed towards the same goal: contemplation." On the retreat to Cassiciacum see Peter Brown, *Augustine of Hippo* (Berkeley, 1967), 115–27.

On monks as "friends in God" see Peter Brown, *The Making of Late Antiquity* (Cambridge, Mass., 1978), 54–80 and David Konstan, *Friendship in the Classical World* (Cambridge, 1997), 161–73. On the complex meaning of *monasterium* see Joseph T. Lienhard, *Paulinus of Nola and Early Western Monasticism* (Cologne, 1977), 58–69.

the first, moreover, these religious communities adopted the code of common property (*Confessions*, 6.14.24):[25]

> Among our group of friends we had had animated discussions of a project: talking with one another we expressed detestation for the storms and troubles of human life, and had almost decided on withdrawing from the crowds and living a life of contemplation. This contemplative leisure we proposed to organize in the following way: everything that we could raise we would put into a common treasury and from everyone's resources would create a single household chest. In sincere friendship nothing would be the private property of this or that individual, but out of the resources of all one treasury would be formed; the whole would belong to each, and everything would belong to everybody.

25. Augustine, *Confessions*, trans. Henry Chadwick (Oxford, 1991). For the experiments in monastic living and their foundation in friendship see Brockwell, "Augustine's Ideal of Monastic Community: A Paradigm for his Doctrine of the Church"; Halliburton, "The Inclination to Retirement—the Retreat of Cassiciacum and the 'Monastery' at Thagaste"; Lawless, ix; Markus, 160–69 and Dennis E. Trout, "Augustine at Cassiciacum: *Otium Honestum* and the Social Dimensions of Conversion," *Vigiliae Christianae*, 42 (1988), 132–46.

Possidius describes the monastery at Thagaste in his *Life of St. Augustine*, ch. 5 (trans. Mary Magdeleine Muller and Roy J. Deferrari, *Early Christian Biographies*, ed. Roy J. Deferrari in *The Fathers of the Church: A New Translation*, vol. 15 [NP, 1952], 78): "Soon after his ordination as presbyter, Augustine founded a monastery within the Church, and began to live there among the servants of God according to the rule and custom established by the holy Apostles. The principal regulation of the society specified that no one should own anything, but that all things should be held in common and distributed according to personal needs."

As in Rome, Augustine and his friends at Cassiciacum hold all things in common. More successful than the Roman experiment, moreover, withdrawal to Cassiciacum also produces some of Augustine's most important early works. Not surprisingly, these works, like the retreat that sponsors them, bear the imprint of Pythagoreanism.[26]

Augustine's dialogue in two books entitled *De ordine*, for instance, ends its exploration of the orderly arrangement of the universe—a topic explored, as we have seen, in Plato's *Gorgias*—by invoking Pythagoras' authority. "And what has been disclosed almost to our very eyes by you today?" Alypius asks Augustine, "Is it not that venerable and almost divine teaching which is rightly attributed to Pythagoras—in fact, proved to be his?" (2.20.53).[27] And if Augustine is writing works at Cassiciacum that, while wholly in God's service, as he puts it in the *Confessions* (9.4.7), still breathe the atmosphere of the schools, he is simultaneously reading the Psalms—here especially the fourth Psalm—according to those methods of study or *meditatio* familiar from Aulus Gellius' characterization of Pythagorean *disciplina* (9.4.10).[28]

26. For Jerome's similar early attraction to Pythagoreanism see *Against Rufinus, Dogmatic and Polemical Works*, trans. John N. Hritzu in *The Fathers of the Church* (Washington, D.C., 1965), LIII, 3.39–40, esp. 39, quoting Ep. 84.6: "But granted that I made a mistake in my youth and, having been trained in the studies of the philosophers, that is to say, the pagan philosophers, I was ignorant of the Christian doctrines in the beginning of my faith, and I assumed that what I read in Pythagoras and Plato and Empedocles was also contained in the Apostles." And see Elizabeth Clark, *The Origenist Controversy*, 121–51 and 221–27.

27. *Divine Providence and the Problem of Evil: A Translation of St. Augustine's De Ordine*, ed. and trans. Robert P. Russell (New York, 1942). For other echoes of the *Gorgias* in this work, see *Confessions*, trans. Henry Chadwick, 6, 15, and 21.

28. At *De ordine* 2.20.53, Alypius refers to Pythagorean training as *Py-*

Between withdrawing to Cassiciacum and establishing the monastery at Thagaste, Augustine also writes the *De libero arbitrio,* a dialogue in three books about the freedom of the will to make choices. Crucial among the choices we make is the kind of life we choose to live. As discussed in chapter 2, this singularly important choice not only inspired Pythagoras' image of life as a festival but also figured prominently in several of Plato's dialogues, including the *Protagoras,* the *Gorgias,* the *Symposium,* and the *Republic.* Like the Pythagorean figure and the Platonic dialogues, moreover, Augustine's own dialogue rejects both *philotimia* and *philochrēmatia*—what Augustine calls *amor laudis et gloriae,* love of honor and glory, and *affectatio dominandi,* love of ownership (often reduced in translation to "power") (1.8.18).[29] To choose this last kind of life, Augustine explains,

---

thagorae disciplina. On *disciplina* see Jean Leclercq, *The Love of Learning and the Desire for God,* 101–02. For a different view of Augustine's use of this term see Brown, *Augustine of Hippo,* 236–42.

For Augustine's meditation on the Psalms as an instance of *lectio divina* see Brian Stock, *Augustine the Reader: Meditation, Self-Knowledge, and the Ethics of Interpretation* (Cambridge, Mass., 1996), 5–19 and 113–16. On the role of meditation in *lectio divina* see Leclercq, *The Love of Learning and the Desire for God,* 17: "In Christian as well as rabbinical tradition, one cannot meditate anything else but a text, and since this text is the word of God, meditation is the necessary complement, almost the equivalent, of the *lectio divina.* . . . For the ancients, to meditate is to read a text and to learn it 'by heart' in the fullest sense of this expression, that is, with one's whole being: with the body, since the mouth pronounced it, with the memory which fixes it, with the intelligence which understands its meaning, and with the will which desires to put it into practice." See also 71–77.

29. For the Latin text see *Oeuvres de Saint Augustin,* trans. F. J. Thonnard (Paris, 1952), vol. 6; and for the English translation, *On Free Will* in *Augustine: Earlier Writings, The Library of Christian Classics,* trans. John H. S. Burleigh (Philadelphia, 1953). Burleigh claims (107) that "the *De Libero Arbitrio* may be regarded as the high-water mark of his earlier

is to devote oneself to making money (*pecunia*), "which in one word covers all that we lawfully possess (*domini sumus*) and which we have the right (*potestas*) to dispose of by sale or gift" (1.15.32). Whoever is ruled by *affectatio dominandi*, in other words, is driven to accumulate private property.

Indeed, the concept of private property, especially in contrast to common property, pervades Augustine's thinking in this dialogue about the choices we make.[30] For while the choices belong to us individually, the things we choose may be subject to either private or public ownership. The finer things, however, belong to all in common; and finest among them is the truth (2.12.33):

---

works, and the best and fullest exposition of what may be called the peculiarly Augustinian brand of Neoplatonism." Among the traditional opinions concerning the origin of souls in book 4, Augustine includes and rejects the Pythagorean. For a concise statement of this position see Clark, *The Origenist Controversy*, 145: "the notion of souls falling from heaven into bodies on the basis of diversity of merits acquired in a pre-existent life is a 'pagan' teaching derived from Pythagoras, Plato and their disciples, some of whom try to introduce the view 'under the pretext of Christianity.'"

30. The underlying concept of property is evident throughout Augustine's discussion of human psychology, in regard not only to the soul's *affectationes* (e.g., 1.11.22) but also to the operation of the senses (2.7.19): "It is therefore evident that things which we perceive with the bodily senses without causing them to change are by nature quite different from our senses, and consequently are common (*communia*) to us both, because they are not converted and changed into something which is our peculiar and almost private property (*in nostrum proprium et quasi privatum*). . . . By 'our peculiar and private property' (*proprium ergo et quasi privatum*) I mean that which belongs to each of us alone, which each of us perceives by himself alone, which is part of the natural being of each of us severally. By 'common and almost public property' (*commune autem et quasi publicum*) I mean that which is perceived by all sentient beings without its being thereby affected and changed."

Accordingly, you will never deny that there is an unchangeable truth (*veritatem*) which contains everything that is unchangeably true. You will never be able to say that it belongs particularly to you or to me (*tuam vel meam*) or to any man, for it is available and offers itself to be shared by all who discern things immutably true, as if it were some strange mysterious and yet public light. Who would say that what is available to be shared by all reasoning and intelligent persons can be the private property of any of them?

Among these immutable truths held in common is the science of number (2.8.24) and the revelations of Scripture.[31] The will

31. The argument for shared intellectual property that Augustine makes in the *De libero arbitrio* after living in a community of likeminded friends is reformulated in the *Confessions*. Laboring in this later work to account for the multiplicity of interpretations that Scripture engenders so that these partial understandings might serve to strengthen rather than erode a spiritual commonwealth, he turns once again to the Pythagorean notion of common ownership of the truth revealed in Scripture. Of those who would claim some right of private possession, Augustine insists that (12.25.34) "it cannot be merely their private property. If they respect an affirmation because it is true, then it is already both theirs and mine, shared by all lovers of the truth. But their contention that Moses did not mean what I say but what they say, I reject. I do not respect that. . . . for your truth does not belong to me nor to anyone else, but to us all whom you call to share it as a public possession. With terrifying words you warn against regarding it as a private possession, or we may lose it (Matt. 25:14–30). Anyone who claims for his own property what you offer for all to enjoy, and wishes to have exclusive rights to what belongs to everyone, is driven from the common truth to his own private ideas, that is from truth to a lie. For 'he who speaks a lie' speaks 'from his own' (John 8:44)."

See also *De opere monachorum* 25.32 and R. A. Markus, "Vie Monas-

that not only embraces the commonality of these higher goods but also chooses common over private property is itself good. On the other hand (2.18.53), "the will which turns from the unchangeable and common good and turns to its own private good or to anything exterior or inferior, sins." Whereas those Christians who choose the monastic life choose the common ownership of material property, all those who live good Christian lives share whatever is true as their common intellectual property.

As self-proclaimed heir of the double tradition of ancient philosophy and early Christianity, Erasmus could not help but discover *philosophia Christi* among his intellectual belongings. For the commonalities between the philosophical way of life as characterized not only by the Platonic dialogues but also by the late antique literary portraits of Pythagoras and the religious common life as characterized by early Christian writers are virtually inescapable. Indeed, these early Christians, as we have seen, were themselves the intellectual heirs of the ancient philosophical tradition. As we have also seen, the *Adages,* the common repository of this tradition, opens by boldly announcing these same commonalities—an announcement echoed not only in several later adages, as we will see momentarily, but more immediately in the *pythagorae symbola.*

The second adage of Erasmus' collection is actually a collection of adages within a collection, and all are attributed, like the first adage, to Pythagoras. Some of them, not surprisingly, address the notion of friendship. Several, including some of these, address the commonality between Pythagoreanism and Christianity.[32] One of these is the double adage that heads this smaller collection: "Friendship is equality" ("Amicitia aequalitas") and

tique et Ascétisme chez Saint Augustin," *Congresso Internazionale su S. Agostino nel XVI Centenario della Conversione* (Rome, 1987), 119–25.

32. See Margaret Mann Phillips, 383–90.

"A friend is another self" ("Amicus alter ipse"). It concludes by remarking the coincidence between these sentiments and "the law of the Hebrews" which "commands us to love our neighbors as ourselves" (*CWE*, 31, 31). Another is "Sacrificing must be by odd numbers to the gods above, but by even numbers to the gods below," where Erasmus notes that not only Plato and the Pythagoreans but also some early theological writers or *prisci theologici* wonder at the mystical property of numbers (LB, II, 20B; *CWE*, 31, 41). In yet a third, "panem ne frangito" (I.i.2; LB II, 23D; *CWE*, 31, 46)—"Do not break bread"—Erasmus concludes the 1517 version with the observation that Christ, like Pythagoras, sought to preserve *amicitia* among his own followers by instituting the sharing of bread.[33] And a fourth, "Walk not in the pub-

33. On the *Pythagorae symbola* see S. K. Heninger, Jr., "Pythagorean Symbola in Erasmus' *Adagia*," *Renaissance Quarterly*, 21 (1968), 162–65, where Heninger speculates that "these enigmatic preachments, in circulation as early as the Church Fathers, were perhaps the germ of Erasmus' plan for a collection of adages" (162). See also S. K. Heninger, Jr., *Touches of Sweet Harmony: Pythagorean Cosmology and Renaissance Poetics* (San Marino, Calif., 1974), 66 n. 54 and 272–77.

In the *Prolegomena* to the *Adages*, Erasmus identifies the Eucharist with the *koinōnia* among Christ's followers based on His friendship for them and their friendship in turn for one another (LB, II, 7AB; *CWE*, 31, 15): "Or what else does love teach us, except that all things should be common to all? In fact that united in friendship with Christ, glued to Him by the same binding force that holds Him fast to the Father, imitating so far as we may that complete communion by which He and the Father are one, we should also be one with Him. . . . This is signified to us by the mystic bread, brought together out of many grains into one flour, and the draught of wine fused into one liquid from many clusters of grapes."

On the *koinōnia* of the Eucharist and its association with the common meal of the Pythagoreans, see my " 'Between Friends All is Common': The Erasmian Adage and Tradition." On the common meal more generally in the ancient philosophical and literary traditions see Michel

lic highway" ("Per publicam viam ne ambules"), "agrees with the teaching of the Gospel, which recommends us to avoid the broad road where most people walk, and take the narrow way, trodden by few but leading to immortality" (LB, II, 20C; *CWE*, 31, 41).

This last adage is expressly contradicted, however, by another in the same group: "Do not walk outside the public highway" ("Extra publicam viam ne deflectas") (LB, II, 21BC; *CWE*, 31, 42); and this contradiction points to the arguably contradictory enterprise of adding these particular adages, handed down to educate the initiated few, to a collection designed to make the wisdom of the ancient Pythagoreans common property. Meeting this apparent discrepancy head-on, Erasmus takes the opportunity to reaffirm a special rhetorical property of all proverbs (LB, II, 21BC; *CWE*, 31, 42): "We need not be surprised at this contradiction since, as has been rightly laid down, one should speak like the many but think like the few, and yet at the same time there are matters in which it is the part of a skillful man to agree with the multitude, and others in which a good man must entirely differ from it." Here as elsewhere in the *Adages*, in other words, Erasmus invokes the proverb's responsiveness to context. As we have already seen in the *Prolegomena*, this capacity for accommodation distinguishes the proverb as a discursive form.[34]

On the one hand, then, Erasmus seems only too willing to divulge as far as he is able the "private" wisdom of the Pythagoreans; on the other, he can prefer not to share his own scholarly material with literary competitors. In yet another adage included in the *pythagorae symbola*, "Do not sit on the grain measure,"

Jeanneret, *A Feast of Words: Banquets and Table Talk in the Renaissance*, trans. Jeremy Whiteley and Emma Hughes (Chicago, 1991). For Erasmus' reception of these traditions, see esp. 176–85.

34. See above, p. 38.

Erasmus charges a fellow author, Lodovico Ricchieri, with pilfering the property of other collectors for his *Antiquae Lectiones* (*CWE*, 31, 34–35):[35]

> The fact that he nowhere, so far as I could find out, mentioned the name of Giorgio Valla of Volterra, or my name: (although it is probable that he was helped to a certain extent by our collections) I know to have been the result of discretion and not malice; even if, when he is writing about this very precept he asserts that he does not wish to put anything forward which bubbles up in anyone else's work (this is how he talks), and at the same time he produces a good many things which I find in my own *Chiliades*.

Sometimes Erasmus' proprietary feelings toward his literary project get the better of his community-mindedness, calling into question the sentiment with which he ends this same adage. "The value of learning to the public," he concludes somewhat unconvincingly in the wake of his complaint against Ricchieri, "is more important to me than the matter of my own reputation" (*CWE*, 31, 35).

Despite its occasional contradictoriness, the *pythagorae symbola* as a whole testify to both the common bond between Pythagorean and Christian philosophy and the *amicitia* underlying this bond. Later in the first *chilias*, in fact, Erasmus will return not only to this bond but also to the Pythagorean sayings that support it. In "salem et mensam ne praeteream" (I.vi.10; LB II, 225C; *CWE*, 32, 10) he records that the ancient Italian philosopher enjoined his disciples to "transgress not salt and trencher" —an injunction that Origen in his commentary on Matthew invokes to describe Judas' transgression against Christ. On this

35. On this episode see Allen, II, 348n and *CWE*, 31, 34n.

same topic of transgression, yet another adage, "quo transgressus" (III.x.1), rehearses the pseudo-Pythagorean catechism from the *Carmina Aurea* (i.e., "What have I done wrong? What have I accomplished? What have I yet to accomplish?") as a fitting meditation not only for all Christians but particularly for some contemporary monks who are in special need of self-study.[36]

Here as elsewhere, Erasmus distinguishes sharply between the early cenobitic movements he found to share so much with the antique philosophical, especially Pythagorean, life and the monasticism of his own day.[37] The former he describes with reference to the rules of Augustine in his famous letter to Paul Volz cited above: a life "with friends who joined them willingly . . . according to the teaching of the gospel" (Allen, III, 375; *CWE,* 66, 21). In his own day, in contrast, monasteries have all the religious discipline or *disciplina pietatis* of a brothel (Ep. 447, Allen, II, 307; *CWE,* 4, 25).

So corrupt is the contemporary common life that Erasmus writes to a fictitious friend named Lambertus Grunnius to rehearse his recently argued case to another friend against taking monastic vows (Ep. 447). As part of his argument, Erasmus challenges advocates of monasticism who reserve redemption for those living in retirement from the world. For these advocates mistakenly claim "for monks as their private property what

36. On the *Carmina Aurea* see Heninger, *Touches of Sweet Harmony,* 24 and 259–63. Heninger quotes the first English translation of the line in question, translated by Thomas Stanley in 1651, as (261) "how slipt? what Deeds? what duty left undone?" For Aldus' special involvement in the publication of this Pythagorean text see *Touches of Sweet Harmony,* 56 and 63–64 n. 41. The friendship and collaboration between Erasmus and Aldus is the subject of the next chapter. And see Celenza, "Pythagoras in the Renaissance," 673.

37. On Erasmus' view of sixteenth-century monastic culture see, for example, Tracy, *Erasmus of the Low Countries,* 90–94.

belongs in common to every Christian" (Allen, II, 301; *CWE,* 4, 18). To distinguish between monastic life and true Christian living, in other words, Erasmus returns to the familiar issue of property ownership that has informed not only all aspects of this tradition but even the notion of tradition itself. And he insists on the priority of those things traditioned to all Christians equally.

At an even earlier date, on the other hand, Erasmus had argued in favor of monastic withdrawal. Also in the form of a fictitious letter, the *De contemptu mundi* urges the same commonalities as the letter to Grunnius; and it does so while similarly recalling the simplicities of late antique cenobitic living (LB, V, 1261DE; *CWE,* 66, 173):

> Once monasteries were nothing but solitary dwelling places for pious men who disdained the enticements and vices that afflicted human life—more so at that time than now because pagans and Christians lived together—or who, harrowed by cruel persecutions, left the cities and hid in the pathless mountains to meditate (*meditantes*) upon an angelic kind of life. They clothed themselves humbly and ate sparingly so that any soil easily supported them; they spent all their time in sacred hymns, sacred literature, heavenly conversation, pious prayers, or charitable deeds, helping sick and weary travelers to recover their strength or devoting themselves to blameless works in support of needy people. In those times, to be a monk meant nothing more than to be a true Christian, and a monastery was nothing else but a congregation of men united in the true teachings of Christ. There was no rule, every man forged ahead of his own account, so that reins were needed rather than spurs. Friendly and brotherly scolding

> was the utmost punishment for them. Now most
> monasteries are in the midst of worldly affairs and so
> entangled in them that they are no less parted from
> the world than are kidneys from a living body.

Here as in the letter to Grunnius, Erasmus praises early Christian cenobitic living at the expense of sixteenth-century monastic culture. The *disciplina* of these early cenobites, moreover, could just as easily describe Pythagorean *askēsis*. If to be a monk in those days meant nothing else than to be a Christian, to be a Christian, as we have seen above in the *Institutio,* differed little if at all from being a philosopher.[38]

As early as the *De contemptu mundi,* in other words, Erasmus effects the identification between Christianity and philosophy that eventually becomes *philosophia Christi.* And he does so, even at this early stage, with the help of the Pythagoreans. Pythagoras himself is introduced as the prototypical anchorite to prove the pleasures of withdrawal (LB, V, 1254E; *CWE,* 66, 160–61), while Archytas, Pythagoras' student and Plato's teacher, is characterized as "pagan though his thoughts are clearly worthy of a Christian" (LB, V, 1244DE; *CWE,* 66, 142). In this case, Archytas' "Christian thinking" concerns rejecting the wrong kinds of pleasure.

Among the right kinds of pleasure — indeed one of the chief pleasures — of the religious common life outlined in the *De contemptu mundi* is reading, including the kind of reading or studying often called, as we have seen, *meletē* in Greek and *meditatio* in Latin — what Erasmus refers to here more periphrastically as *lecta animo volutare* (LB, V, 1260B; *CWE,* 66, 170). Among the

---

38. On Erasmus' advocacy of asceticism in the classical sense see Alan W. Reese, " 'So Outstanding an Athlete of Christ': Erasmus and the Significance of Jerome's Asceticism," *Erasmus of Rotterdam Society Yearbook,* 18 (1998), 104–17.

monks' reading material, moreover, are the works of classical antiquity.[39] Anticipating the *Adages*, Erasmus refers to these works as "old friends." In stark contrast to the *Adages,* however, he discourages the young reader from approaching these old friends in the spirit of friendship (LB, V, 1260C; *CWE,* 66, 170):

> And if you cannot be parted from old friends forever, you may ever go back to them at times when you have leisure, but in such a manner that you are their rival (*rivalem*), not their associate (*convictorem*). For there is among them that captive woman, barbarian but of honest mien, whom you will take (*raptam*) as your wife instead of keeping her as a concubine, once you have cut her hair and trimmed her nails.

Under pressure in his earlier works from the biblical figure of the *mulier captiva,* as we have seen in some detail in chapter 1, Erasmus here understands the classical literary tradition as property appropriated from an enemy. With the publication of the *Adages,* as we have also seen, Erasmus reconfigures the traditionary relation in Pythagorean terms as property held in common among friends.[40] Thus reconfigured, as we will now see, the traditioning of commonly held property Pythagorean-style offers a further challenge to Erasmus' thinking in particular about intellectual, and especially literary property.

39. See Erika Rummel, "Quoting Poetry Instead of Scripture: Erasmus and Eucherius on *Contemptus Mundi,*" *Bibliotèque d'Humanisme et Renaissance,* 45 (1983), 503–09. On the composition of this work see *CWE,* 66, xliv–xlviii and 130–34.

40. Which is not to say that Erasmus never again refers to the rivalry between pagan and Christian authors. See, for instance, the dedicatory letter to the *Institutio principis Christiani,* Ep. 393 (1516), where he names Isocrates his model and rival (Allen, II, 207; *CWE,* 3, 250).

6

Intellectual Property and the *Adages*

Arguably the single hottest literary property of the first quarter of the sixteenth century, Erasmus' *Adagiorum chiliades* helped to secure the fame and fortune of Europe's two most powerful printing houses during this time, that of Aldo Manuzio in Venice and Johann Froben in Basel. The Aldine edition of the *Adages,* by Erasmus' own account the product of friendship and close collaboration, appeared under its new title in 1508, vastly expanding and revising the Paris *Collectanea* of 1500. Seven years later, the second edition, again revised and expanded, launched the longstanding friendship and commercial partnership between Erasmus and Froben, his most successful northern publisher.[1] These publication events belong to a larger picture of the rapidly changing intellectual and material landscape inhabited by sixteenth-century Europeans—changes that had an especially jolting impact on their experience as readers.

For the published *Adages* represents not only an artifact that many more people could own because of the new technology

---

1. On the evolution of the *Adages* through its several editions see Margaret Mann Phillips, *The "Adages" of Erasmus.* On the importance of this publication event to the careers of both author and publisher see Martin Lowry, *The World of Aldus Manutius: Business and Scholarship in Renaissance Venice* (Cornell, 1979), 151, 228, and 263. On the role of these publishing houses in Erasmus' career, see Peter G. Bietenholz, "Ethics and Early Printing: Erasmus' Rules for the Proper Conduct of Authors," *Humanities Association Review,* 26 (1975), 180–95, Jardine, *Erasmus, Man of Letters* and Tracy, *Erasmus of the Low Countries,* 43–46. For the popularity of the *Adages,* see Ep. 492, Allen, II, 388–89; *CWE,* 4, 135.

of printing, but it also, in ways that worried some of Erasmus'
colleagues, made these many book-owners at once proprietors
of a classical heritage that had previously been the intellectual
property of very few. Both the resolute mission of one author to
divulge the wisdom of the ancients and the anxiety of the few
about this divulgence are recorded in the *Adages* themselves. In
"Festina lente"—"Make haste slowly"—Erasmus recalls the re-
luctance of one acquaintance to share his manuscripts in this
effort on the grounds that "everything is now becoming public
property from which scholars hitherto had been able to secure
the admiration of the common people" (LB, II, 405EF; *CWE*,
33, 15).[2] Denied access to this colleague's private property, Erasmus outspokenly upholds the need to subordinate one's personal
stake to a common enterprise designed to benefit an entire community of readers (e.g., "Herculei labores," LB II, 715E–716B).
And his first biographer and friend, Beatus Rhenanus, corrobo-
rates Erasmus' commitment to this enterprise. "When he was
about to publish the *Adages*," Beatus remembers, "certain scholars said to him, 'Erasmus, you are divulging our secrets.' But he
was desirous that these be accessible to all so that they might
attain to complete scholarship."[3]

The publication of the *Adages,* in other words, reflects chang-

2. On book-sharing as an element of friendship see Martin Lowry,
Nicholas Jenson and the Rise of Venetian Publishing in Renaissance Europe
(Oxford, 1991), 31–35 and Natalie Zemon Davis, "Books as Gifts in
Sixteenth-Century France," *Transactions of the Royal Historical Society,* 33
(1983), 69–88.

3. "The Life of Erasmus by Beatus Rhenanus" in *Christian Human-
ism and the Reformation: Selected Writings,* ed. and trans. John C. Olin
(New York, 1965), 47–48; for the Latin see Allen, I, 67 and cf. I.i.2, LB,
II, 17AB; *CWE,* 31, 35. See also John F. D'Amico, *Theory and Practice in
Renaissance Textual Criticism: Beatus Rhenanus Between Conjecture and
History* (Berkeley, 1988), esp. 47–55.

ing attitudes and practices regarding property. As we have already seen in some detail in the previous chapters, these attitudes and practices were complex. As we will now see, Erasmus not only understood their complexity but actually exploited it in the composition of this most popular sixteenth-century book. While material changes unquestionably exerted their pressures on these events, it is rather the issues concerning intellectual property that most preoccupied Erasmus.[4] And what better forum for such a preoccupation than a compendium of proverbs.

For the proverb is, as the *Prolegomena* to the 1508 edition argues, a literary form that by definition defies individual ownership. Passed down from generation to generation and around

4. For the impact of material changes on the history of the book see, for instance, Roger Chartier and Daniel Roche, "New Approaches to the History of the Book" in *Constructing the Past: Essays in Historical Methodology*, eds. Jacques Le Goff and Pierre Nora (Cambridge, 1985), 198–214; Joyce Coleman, *Public Reading and the Reading Public in Late Medieval England and France* (Cambridge, 1996); Robert Darnton, "What is the History of Books?" and "First Steps Toward a History of Reading" in *The Kiss of Lamourette: Reflections in Cultural History* (New York, 1990), 107–35 and 154–87; S. L. Hindman, ed., *Printing the Written Word: The Social History of Books, c. 1450–1520* (Ithaca, 1992).

It is a commonly held view that the notions of literary property and its corollary, copyright, are the offspring of the printing press. Before Erasmus' day, as one scholar puts it, "the owner of a book also possessed legal rights to its contents. In other words, an author's rights passed to the owner of the book, which indicates that there was no distinction between physical and intellectual property rights" (Leonardus Vytautas Gerulaitis, *Printing and Publishing in Fifteenth-Century Venice* [Chicago, 1976], 32). For a slightly different formulation, see Rudolf Hirsch, *Printing, Selling and Reading 1450–1550* (Wiesbaden, 1967), 8–9; for disagreement, see F. D. Prager, "The Early Growth and Influence of Intellectual Property," *Journal of the Patent Office Society*, 34 (1952), 106–40.

On the status of intellectual property in Roman law see *Justinian's Institutes*, trans. Peter Birks and Grant McLeod (Ithaca, 1987), II.1.25–34 and Prager, 109, 114–17.

from place to place, proverbs or adages encode over time and space a collective wisdom that belongs equally to all members of a community. On just this feature of proverbial statement, Erasmus quotes Quintilian (LB II, 7DE; *CWE*, 31, 16; cf. *Institutio Oratoria*, 5.11.37–42): "Popular sayings which command general assent will also be found not without value as supporting material. . . . Those things too which command general assent seem to be, as it were, common property from the fact that they have no certain author."[5] Precisely because they constitute a common store, then, adages or proverbs invite reflection on the nature of private property, especially private intellectual property. With the coming of age of printing, moreover, authors like Erasmus had more reason than ever to reflect.

Indeed, it is in Venice during the last years of the fifteenth and first years of the sixteenth century—the where and when of the first edition of the *Adages*—that laws regarding intellectual property, including copyright, begin their slow but continual evolution toward the modern legal institutions that form so familiar a part of our own landscape.[6] In 1486 a Venetian author,

5. On this feature of the proverb, especially as it is treated in the *Prolegomena*, see my " 'Between Friends All is Common': The Erasmian Adage and Tradition," 408–11.

6. On the early history of intellectual property, especially copyright, see John Feather, "From Rights in Copies to Copyright: The Recognition of Authors' Rights in English Law and Practice in the Sixteenth and Seventeenth Centuries," *Cardozo Arts and Entertainment Law Journal*, 10 (1992), 455–73; Paul Goldstein, *Copyright's Highway: The Law and Lore of Copyright from Gutenberg to the Celestial Jukebox* (New York, 1994); F. D. Prager, "The Early Growth and Influence of Intellectual Property"; A. J. K. Robinson, "The Evolution of Copyright, 1476–1776," *The Cambrian Law Review*, 22 (1991), 55–77; Mark Rose, *Authors and Owners: The Invention of Copyright* (Cambridge, Mass., 1993); Mladen Vukmir, "The roots of Anglo-American intellectual property law in Roman law," *IDEA: The Journal of Law and Technology*, 32 (1992), 123–54.

Marcantonio Sabellico, requests from the Venetian Council the first copyright, termed a privilege or *privilegium*, for his history of Venice, the *Rerum Venetarum Libri XXXIII*. Six years later, Pier Francesco da Ravenna, requesting a similar privilege for his *Foenix*, a study of artificial memory, is granted his copyright by the Council on the grounds not only that the community is entitled to a work that serves the common good (*ad universalem commoditatem et utilitatem*) but also that its author is entitled to the fruits of his own labor (*fructus laborum et vigiliarum suarum*). Four years later, in 1496, the Council grants Aldo Manuzio, Erasmus' publisher, a patent for his ancient Greek type on the same grounds—entitlement to the fruits of time and money spent on an enterprise so beneficial to their community, the illustrious city of Venice.[7]

In the years following, Aldus continues to look to the Council to protect his intellectual property through patents and copyrights in the form of privileges. In 1498 he applies for copyright for editions of several ancient Greek authors, including Demosthenes, Hermogenes, Plutarch, and Xenophon; in 1500, for the

7. On the early privilege-system, especially in Venice, during the last years of the fifteenth and first years of the sixteenth century, see Elizabeth Armstrong, *Before Copyright: The French Book-Privilege System 1498–1526* (Cambridge, 1990), esp. 1–6; Carlo Castellani, *La Stampa in Venezia dalla sua origine alla morte di Aldo Manuzio Seniore* (Trieste, 1889; rpt. 1973); Ruth Chavasse, "The First Known Author's Copyright, September 1486, In the Context of a Humanist Career," *Bulletin of the John Rylands University Library of Manchester*, 69 (1986), 11–37; R. Fulin, "Primi privilegi di stampa in Venezia," *Archivio veneto*, 1 (1871), 160–64; Leonardus Vytautas Gerulaitis, *Printing and Publishing in Fifteenth-Century Venice*, esp. 33–46; Rudolf Hirsch, *Printing, Selling and Reading 1450–1550*, 78–103.

For the texts of these first *privilegia*, see R. Fulin, "Documenti per servire alla Storia della Tipografia veneziana," *Archivio veneto*, 23 (1882), 84–212, esp. 102 (to Sabellico and Pier Francesco da Ravenna) and 120 and 136 (to Aldo Manuzio). See also Castellani, 69–78, esp. 71–72.

letters of Catherine of Siena. In 1501 he receives a patent for his italic type, and in 1502 his request for protection from infringements on this privilege earns him a ten-year patent on both Greek and italic types.[8]

By 1507, the year before he and Erasmus collaborate on bringing out the first edition of the *Adages*, Aldus has already been embroiled in at least two lawsuits over intellectual property and has in fact just prevailed in one of them—a major litigation with a competitor over the pirating of a number of Aldine texts. His adversary, Filippo Giunti, (it seems) refrained from further copyright infringement, avoiding Aldus' titles, but was less compliant on the issue of patent, continuing to copy the fashionable italic type.[9]

It is, then, to a Venice at once anointed with the commer-

8. For the texts of the *privilegia* see Castellani, 75–77 and Fulin, "Documenti," 136, 141–42, 144–45, 149–50; for discussion see Castellani, 35–60; Gerulaitis, 40–45; Hirsch, 85–86; Lowry, *The World of Aldus Manutius*, 111–54; Robert Proctor, *The Printing of Greek in the Fifteenth Century* (Oxford, 1900; rpt. Hildesheim, 1966), 110–14 and N. G. Wilson, *From Byzantium to Italy: Greek Studies in the Italian Renaissance* (Baltimore, 1992), 124–56.

On the overlapping early history of copyright and patent law see Prager, 122–40 and Rose, 45. On the potential for conflict see Lowry, 89–90.

9. On these lawsuits see Lowry, *The World of Aldus Manutius*, 156–58, concluding, "Success in this case, which was presumably decided some time in the late autumn of 1507, must have given Aldus real encouragement as he prepared to resume operations. Planning appears to have been in hand for some time: [Johannes] Cuno reported before the end of December 1506, that preliminary work on the texts of Plato and Plutarch was being discussed, and when Erasmus made his famous approach to Aldus on 28 October of the following year, he never doubted that the company was in business though it had not produced an edition for nearly two years."

On Johannes Cuno of Nuremberg (1463–1513) see D'Amico, 47–48, esp. n. 34 and Wilson, 148.

cial spirit of the young printing industry and exercised in the newly developing legal protocols of intellectual property that Erasmus comes in 1508 with the express intention of publishing his *Adages*. According to Beatus Rhenanus, "When work on the *Adagia* was completed, he wrote to Aldus Manutius to ask if he wished to undertake the printing of the book. The latter replied that he would do so with pleasure. Erasmus then moved to Venice. . . and he received him as his guest in the home of his father-in-law, Andrea Asolani. . . . Nor was his stay in Venice a brief one."[10] Thus begins the mutually profitable friendship that Erasmus commemorates in one of the longest and best-known adages, "Festina lente." Indeed, Erasmus, in collaboration with his friend and publisher, rearranges and expands the earlier edition, the Paris *Collectanea* of 1500, with an eye to foregrounding not only *amicitia* or friendship but the relation between friendship and wealth, material and intellectual. [11] In doing so, as we will see, Erasmus explores the claims of author, publisher and reader as heir to the so-called classical tradition, the intellectual legacy of Greek and Roman antiquity.

Three adages in the rearranged and expanded edition take on special significance, and all three take up the theme of property, especially intellectual property. The first, of course, is our "Amicorum communia omnia"—"Friends hold all things in common" (LB II, 13F–14F; *CWE*, 31, 29–30). The ninety-fourth adage in the *Collectanea*, as we have seen, it is here moved to initial position, thereby introducing not only the first thousand or *chilias prima* but the entire collection of over three thousand proverbs.[12] Relying in the *Collectanea* on only the briefest allu-

10. Olin, 37–38; Allen, I, 60.

11. See my " 'Between Friends All is Common': The Erasmian Adage and Tradition."

12. While Margaret Mann Phillips notes the relocation of the other

sions to Terence and Plato, this introductory adage is expanded in 1508 both to include other Greek and Latin authors, including Euripides, Aristotle, Menander, Cicero, Martial, and Plutarch, and to feature Pythagoras. So critical is the testimony of Pythagoras as the reputed source of this saying that when Erasmus reworks the Aldine edition for publication by Froben in 1515 he further expands the witnesses to the ancient philosopher's authority.[13] To Cicero (*De legibus* 1.12.34) and Diogenes Laertius (8.10) he adds Aulus Gellius, who records in his *Noctes Atticae* (1.9.12) that Pythagoras was not only the father of this saying but also the first philosopher of common—in contrast to private— property; and as such, Erasmus infers, he is arguably the father of *coenobium* or cenobitic monasticism.[14]

---

two—"Festina lente" and "Herculei labores"—she leaves this one out of the account; and while she observes that the second and third deal with the "compilation and publication of the *Adages* themselves," she does not touch on the theme of intellectual property (70).

On the first adage see also *ASD* II-I, 84–87.

13. On the important role of the *Adages* in launching Erasmus' association with the Froben press, see Lowry, *The World of Aldus Manutius*, 273 and Margaret Mann Phillips, 96. For Beatus Rhenanus on this publishing event see Olin, 41; Allen, I, 63.

14. Again, Margaret Mann Phillips notes the importance of Pythagoras' authority in the *Adages*, alongside Plato's and Aristotle's, but does not pursue the reasons for it (94). See also S. K. Heninger, Jr., "*Pythagorean Symbola* in Erasmus' *Adagia*," esp. 165, n. 15, where he cites the place of the *carmina aurea*, falsely attributed to Pythagoras, in Aldus' grammars.

On the Pythagorean origins of cenobitic monasticism see my "*Koinōnia* and the Friendship between Rhetoric and Religion."

Not incidentally, the Aldine Press greatly contributed to the accessibility of Pythagoras' teaching by publishing not only his sayings but also Iamblichus and Philostratus. See Castellani, 41 and Lowry, *The World of Aldus Manutius*, 111, 119, and 148. Both Aulus Gellius and Diogenes Laertius were already available from Nicholas Jenson's press, the former in 1472, the latter in 1475. See Lowry, *Nicholas Jenson and the Rise of Venetian*

But the opening proverb introduces not only the first thousand adages as well as the entire collection of over three thousand; it also introduces, as we have seen, the *pythagorae symbola*, the precepts of Pythagoras, that constitute altogether the first thirty-nine adages of both the 1508 and all subsequent editions (LB, II, 14F–25E). Erasmus, in other words, begins his compendium of ancient wisdom by establishing the Pythagorean legacy of common property as at once material and intellectual. Friends in the Pythagorean sense share not only a common store of material goods but a common stock of proverbial sayings. And it is by no means incidental that this philosopher of friendship, as Pythagoras was often called, should choose the proverb as the preeminent discursive form. For like friendship as a social *praxis*, proverbial statement as a discursive *praxis* forges a unity out of the experience of the many.[15]

By moving the ninety-fourth proverb of the *Collectanea* to initial position in the Aldine *Adagiorum chiliades*, Erasmus initiates a case for the reader of the newly published book as heir to the intellectual tradition of antiquity. In contrast to the figure from Exodus (12:35–36) of the Israelites despoiling their enemies, as we have seen in chapter 1, the Pythagorean adage allows

Publishing in Renaissance Europe, 242, 244. The Aldine Press also brought out Philostratus' *Life of Apollonius of Tyana* with Latin translation by Alamanno Rinuccini (1501–04). See Wilson, *From Byzantium to Italy*, 137: "The first book to be set up in type was not one of the most significant. It is difficult to know why Aldus interested himself in Philostratus' *Life of Apollonius of Tyana.* . . . Neither Aldus nor More could be expected to take much interest in an ascetic Pythagorean of the first century, who presents an intriguing figure for students of the history of religion in antiquity."

15. See my " 'Between Friends All is Common': The Erasmian Adage and Tradition." For Pythagoras as the philosopher of friendship, see, for instance, Iamblichus, *On the Pythagorean Life*, 69–70, 229–30.

Erasmus to figure the tradition about to be divulged as the common treasury of intellectual wealth belonging equally to a like-minded community of friends. Like the first initiates at Croton, moreover, this broadly European intellectual community not only does not deplete the common store through use but, through sound investment in the form of their own literary production, actually leaves it enriched for the next generation. Under the favorable auspices of the first adage (LB, II, 13F), in other words, Erasmus signals to the reader the rights and obligations implicit in sharing the intellectual wealth of antiquity.[16]

By beginning his collection with this particular proverb, Erasmus also demonstrates the enormous power of the editor-author to dispose or arrange inherited material. Not surprisingly, he not only uses this strategy again but does so in comparable circumstances. Numbering 196 in the *Collectanea*, "Festina lente"— "Make haste slowly"—is moved in the Aldine edition to introduce the second thousand or *chilias secunda*. It is also greatly expanded, maturing, as it were, into one of the longest and most popular adages of the entire collection.[17] And it too, retrieving

16. As early as 1498 in a letter to Christian Northoff (Ep. 61, Allen, I, 183; *CWE* I, 127), Erasmus writes about *bonae literae* that *"solas illas esse proprias hominis opes, neque dari a fortuna neque eripi posse; usu augeri, non minui."* See Tracy, *Erasmus of the Low Countries*, 28 and Goldstein, 14.

17. Called simply *Matura* in the *Collectanea*, this adage addresses the importance of *maturity* not only in the arena of scholarship but also of politics. See LB, II, 399 and Margaret Mann Phillips, 174. And see Roland Bainton, *Erasmus of Christendom* (New York, 1969; rpt. 1982), 83–85; Antoine Compagnon, *La seconde main: ou le travail de la citation* (Paris, 1979), 267–70 and Thomas M. Greene, "Erasmus's 'Festina Lente': Vulnerabilities of the Humanist Text," *Mimesis, From Mirror to Method: Augustine to Descartes,* eds. John D. Lyons and Stephen G. Nichols, Jr. (Hanover, N.H., 1982), 132–48.

the theme that inaugurated the first thousand, presses forward on the issue of intellectual property. Like "Amicorum communia omnia," moreover, and in keeping with the ancient legacy handed down by the *Adages*, "Festina lente" situates its reflections on property in the larger context of political philosophy.

Whereas the opening adage adds the authority of Plato and Aristotle to that of Pythagoras in establishing the community of friends as the paradigm for the republic or commonwealth, "Festina lente" begins with the consequences of undue haste and sloth in the political arena, in the actions of men of state. For in this arena, the decisions of the one affect the material well-being of the many. So fundamental is this common wisdom to sound government that two of the most praiseworthy men of state (and emperors no less), Octavius Augustus and Titus Vespasian, take it as their motto (LB, II, 399B; *CWE,* 33, 5). Vespasian even goes so far as to have it impressed on the coins of the realm (LB, II, 399EF; *CWE,* 33, 5):

> Vespasian's approval of our maxim can easily be inferred from very ancient coins issued by him, one of which I was allowed to inspect by Aldo Manuzio. . . . The design (*character*) of the coin was as follows. One side showed the head of Vespasian with an inscription, the other an anchor, the central shaft of which had a dolphin coiled round it. Now the only meaning conveyed by this symbol (*symboli*) is that favorite maxim of the emperor Augustus "Make haste slowly"; and this we learn from the ancient texts relating to hieroglyphs (*monimenta literarum hieroglyphicarum*).

Already recognizable to the reader of the Aldine *Adages* as the mark of its publisher, the symbol of anchor and dolphin is here introduced as an object of material wealth inscribed with political wisdom and handed down to this same publisher, Aldus Manutius. Inscribing this apparently straightforward description of an inscription within an essay about publishing as part of a larger collection of proverbs representing the common intellectual wealth of antiquity, Erasmus prepares his reader to appreciate in the remainder of the essay the complex interplay of a number of related transfers or *translationes*.

First is the transfer from visual to verbal or literary symbol, a *translatio* effected by the hieroglyph itself. For this ancient form of writing, Erasmus explains immediately following the description, is a kind of drawing or engraving (*figura* or *scalptura*) that resembles the proverb as characterized both in the *Prolegomena* to the entire collection and in the opening of this same essay— an opening that recapitulates the general introduction (LB, II, 397CE and 399F–400A; see also 3B). Like hieroglyphs, proverbs are often enigmatic. And like proverbs, hieroglyphs condense a more copious ancient wisdom (LB, II, 6DE; *CWE,* 31, 14). Being at once enigmatic, hieroglyphic and proverbial, the concentrated symbol of dolphin and anchor must be diluted for public consumption.

In the form of a detailed explanation of the various parts of the symbol—circle, dolphin, and anchor—this dilution entails a journey through mythology, natural history, geometry, and physics. Finally returning to politics, Erasmus reiterates that "this saying, Make haste slowly, arose in the heart of ancient philosophy; whence it was called into their service by two of the most highly esteemed of all Roman emperors, one of whom used it as a device (*adagionis*) the other as an emblem (*insignium*), so well did it agree with the character and disposition of both" (LB, II, 402BC; *CWE,* 33, 9). Once back in the political arena, however, Erasmus effectively works his own transition to the next crucial *translatio.* "And now," he continues (LB, II, 402BC; *CWE,* 33, 9) it has passed to Aldo Manuzio, citizen of Rome, as a kind of heir in the third generation (*ceu tertium haeredem*). . . . Nor do I think this symbol was more illustrious then, when it was stamped on the imperial coinage and suffered the wear and tear of circulation as it passed from one merchant to another, than it is now, when in every nation, even outside the limits of any Christian empire, it spreads and wins recognition, it is held fast and prized in company with books of all kinds in both the ancient languages, by all who are devoted to the cult of liberal studies.

Formerly the property of Augustus and Vespasian, the symbol now belongs to Aldus (cf. 407D); and with this inheritance comes the complementary passing or transfer from material to intellectual property—from mercantile negotiations enabled by such coins as the one of Vespasian now in Aldus' possession to the circulation of knowledge enabled by easier access to such printed books as the *Adages* itself. Proving himself a responsible heir, Aldus not only maintains but increases the value of his inheritance.

With this inheritance from Vespasian to Aldus, in other words, comes the passing of preeminence from politics to scholarship. In the course of this essay, that is, Erasmus skillfully reinvests the traditional complementarity between *translatio imperii* and its corollary, *translatio studii*. The transfer of political power from one culture to another—say, from Egypt to Greece or Greece to Rome—routinely involves the appropriation not only of the vanquished culture's material wealth by the victors, but also its intellectual wealth, usually in the form of literary and artistic production. On this occasion, however, Erasmus invokes a different kind of *translatio:* namely, the transfer from *imperium* to *studium*.[18] For the achievements of an Aldus, Erasmus insists, surpass those of a Ptolemy. Statesmen like Ptolemy merely widen the material boundaries of their empires, while Aldus extends the intellectual community; and as for the imperial prerogative of building librairies, between Ptolemy and Aldus there is no competition (LB, II, 403A; *CWE*, 33, 10):

> however loudly you may sing the praises of those men who by their valour protect or even extend the boundaries of their country, they are active at best in worldly things and constrained within narrow limits. But he who restores a literature in ruins (almost a harder task than to create one) is engaged on a thing sacred and immortal, and works for the benefit not of one province but of all nations everywhere and of all succeeding ages. Last but not least, this was in old days the privilege of princes, among whom Ptolemy won special glory, although his library was contained within the narrow walls of his own palace. Aldus is building a library which knows no walls save those of the world itself.

Heir to the power and prestige of the political ruler, the scholar-publisher inherits as well an obligation to protect and even enlarge his estate for his own beneficiaries. According to Erasmus, Aldus takes on this obligation with unremitting zeal, working day and night to assure that his legacy to the growing community of like-minded students of antiquity survives intact.

The estate itself Erasmus identifies as literary property or *su-*

18. For the more customary parallel transfers of politics and literary culture see, for instance, *Antibarbari, CWE*, 23, 24 and 97. On the relation in Roman law between *translatio* and *traditio* see Fritz Schultz, *Classical Roman Law* (Oxford, 1951), 343–44.

pellex literaria (LB, II, 402D); and Aldus' goal in regard to this property is nothing less than full restoration of past damage and loss. Aldus promises to hand down an ancient literary tradition that is once again complete, genuine and uncorrupted (*& integra, & syncera, puraque*); or, as Erasmus adds, one so restored that none of its heirs any longer feels any part of his literary heritage — again, his literary property or *supellex literaria* — missing (*& plenum habeant & emendatum, nullamque jam literariae supellectilis partem quisquam disideret*) (402E).[19]

Introducing the second thousand in the first Aldine edition, "Festina lente" pays tribute to its publisher. In the well-known addition to this adage in the sixth edition (LB, II, 403B-406B; *CWE*, 33, 10-15), Aldus' dedication to the commonwealth of letters is contrasted with the thoroughly private, monetary aims of the corrupt Northern printers or *sordidi typographi*, whose greed is responsible for the degradation of *res literaria*. Without laws to restrain them, these publishers rush their works into print and thereby harm their readers. Not only do they sell these readers corrupted editions, but they also flood the market with worthless works of the latest writers or *neoterici*, thereby distracting readers from those ancient authors or *veteri* who preside over the various fields of learning.

Coinciding with this corruption, moreover, is the loss of community feeling among those in the printing industry. In the 1526 version of this adage, Erasmus recalls nostalgically his days at the Aldine press when friends held their literary property in common (LB, II, 406BC; *CWE*, 33, 14):

19. On *supellex* see above, pp. 22-24. On Holland as famous for its *supellex domestica* see "Auris Batava," LB, II, 1084E.
Erasmus also uses the term *res literaria* (LB, II, 402F, 403B, 406A; *CWE*, 33, 10 and 15), here translated as "the cause of literature" but also fairly understood as "literary property" with the emphasis on property that has sustained damage.

When I, a Dutchman, was in Italy, preparing to publish my book of *Proverbs,* all the learned men there had offered me unsought authors not yet published in print who they thought might be of use to me and Aldus had nothing in his treasure-house that he did not share (*communicaret*) with me. Johannes Lascaris did the same, so did Battista Egnazio, Marco Musuro, Frate Urbano. I felt the benefit of kindness from some people I knew neither by sight nor name. . . . Just consider what advantages I should have lost, had not scholars supplied me with texts in manuscript.

Almost twenty years later, Erasmus laments the loss of both his colleagues and the common enterprise in the service of a community of readers. To remedy such loss, he recommends public assistance to those who labor for this public good; and one labor especially worthy of assistance is the correction, publication, and translation into Latin of John Chrysostom—a labor Erasmus himself eventually undertakes.[20] Until princes "on our side of the Alps" support such projects, Erasmus argues, the Froben serpents will lag behind the Aldine dolphin (LB, II, 405F-406A; *CWE,* 33, 15).

The second thousand of the first Aldine edition, then, is introduced by an adage featuring Aldus in the role of scholar-publisher—a role in which he figures not only as heir to the most valuable of properties, the literary tradition of antiquity, but also as trustee or guardian of this intellectual wealth on behalf of a larger community. The enterprise, Erasmus claims, is a labor worthy of Hercules—what he calls in this adage a *Her-*

20. See Rudolf Pfeiffer, *History of Classical Scholarship, 1300–1850* (Oxford, 1976), 78.

culanum mehercule facinus (402F). With the introduction of the third thousand, however, Erasmus transfers this qualification from the efforts of the scholar-publisher to those of the scholarly editor-author, or, in other words, from Aldus to himself.

Our third case of strategic relocation involves the equally well-known "Herculei labores"—"The labors of Hercules"— which, numbering thirteen in the *Collectanea* and comprised of a single sentence, Erasmus moves to initial position of the third *chilias* or thousand in the Aldine edition (LB, II, 707D–717B; *CWE*, 34, 167–82). Thus relocated, this adage acquires the status of companion piece to the two other introductory adages already discussed, "Amicorum communia omnia" and "Festina lente"; and as their companion, it joins the ongoing conversation about intellectual, especially literary, property—here one special piece of literary property, the *Adages*. For the focus of this adage is significantly neither Aldus Manutius, who appears only long enough to supply Erasmus with one of the best libraries of ancient texts in the world, nor the restoration of the entire ancient literary tradition, but Erasmus' own labors in the service of compiling for his readers this common treasury of proverbial sayings that constitute no small part of the intellectual wealth of antiquity.

Setting this difference in relief, however, are some noteworthy commonalities. Like the other two adages, this one begins by applying the saying to the political arena—here the ruler's often unappreciated labors in the interest of the ruled (LB, II, 709AB; *CWE*, 34, 169–70). To support this claim, Erasmus adduces both the biblical story of Joseph and the testimony of Philo Judaeus. As in the other adages, moreover, in this one *imperium* soon gives way to *studium*, where the cultural property at issue is once again literary. This time Erasmus effects the transfer or *translatio* from politics to scholarship with the contention that "if any human toils deserve to be awarded the epithet 'Herculean,' it

seems to belong in the highest degree to those at least who devote their efforts to restoring the monuments of ancient and true
literature. Incomparable as are the labours they undertake on account of the incredible difficulty of the subject, they arouse none
the less the greatest unpopularity among the common herd"
(LB, II, 709DE; *CWE*, 34, 170). The many-headed Hydra that
threatens such heroic service, however, is not, as we might be
inclined to think, the recalcitrance of the subject matter; on the
contrary, it is the *invidia* of the hypercritical reader. The writer's
Herculean battle, in other words, is with the monstrous ingrati-
tude of his reading public.[21]

Understanding that in some circumstances the best offense is
a good defense, Erasmus devotes the bulk of this essay to defending his own literary practices in composing the *Adages*, not,
as he assures his audience, "to boast of my intelligence or ad-
vertize my own industry, but to make my reader (*lectorem*) more

21. The earliest form of this adage in the *Collectanea* reads *Proverbio
dicuntur, qui aliis quidem utiles, auctori preter invidiam nihil adferunt.*

On the ungrateful reader see Ep. 396, *CWE*, 3, 262–63, where Erasmus
also refers to the task of editing Jerome as Herculean. In this instance,
however, the monstrosity of the task characterizes the material and not
the reader (263): "And so I despised all the difficulties, and like a modern
Hercules I set out on my most laborious but most glorious campaign,
taking the field almost unaided against all the monsters of error. I cannot
think that Hercules consumed as much energy in taming a few monsters
as I did in abolishing so many blunders. And I conceive that not a little
more advantage will accrue to the world from my work than from his
labours which are on the lips of all men." Cf. Ep. 334, *CWE*, 3, 97 and Ep.
335, *CWE*, 3, 107.

On this adage see Virginia W. Callahan, "The Erasmus-Hercules
Equation in the Emblems of Alciati," *The Verbal and the Visual: Essays in
Honor of William Sebastian Heckscher*, eds. Karl-Ludwig Selig and Elizabeth Sears (New York, 1990), 41–53 and Jardine, 41–45 and 67–73. Her
final chapter touches on the issue of literary property. See 164–69, esp. the
section entitled "Textual Theft: A Footnote on Ownership," 168–69.

sympathetic (*aequiorem*)" (LB, II, 710C; *CWE*, 34, 171). In judging the *Adages*, the equitable or fair-minded reader—the *lector aequus* (cf. 715E)—will consider the particular, even peculiar, challenges facing the author of such a work—challenges that make unusual demands on his powers of invention, disposition and elocution.[22]

Behind Erasmus' portrait of the judgmental reader, moreover, is the critic of the *Ars Poetica,* Horace's handbook for decorous reading as well as writing. Like Homeric epic in its large scale and common themes (*Ars Poetica,* 347–60), the *Adages* deserves pardon from its readers for any minor failings that result from the faults of a craftsmanship rendered fallible by the inherent imperfections of human nature (LB, II, 712CD; *CWE*, 34, 175). On the other hand, the reader of the *Adages,* like that of the Homeric epics according to Horace, has every right to hold the writer responsible for the principles of his art. One such principle is literary economy or *oeconomia,* which entails both selecting the most appropriate details and arranging them for the maximum artistic effect.[23] Just as Homer does not rehearse the entire Trojan War from the first to the last episode, so Erasmus carefully culls and arranges the many available citations of a given adage. And here Erasmus defends his craftsmanship by

22. On Erasmus' quest for the *lector aequus* see my *Hermeneutics and the Rhetorical Tradition,* 1–3, 70–78, 100.

During conversation, Professor Annabel Patterson suggested that Erasmus' defensiveness here about his haste offers another point of correspondence between this adage opening the third thousand and "Festina lente," which opens the second.

23. On the Horatian principles see Wesley Trimpi, "The Meaning of Horace's *Ut Pictura Poesis," Journal of the Warburg and Courtauld Institute,* 36 (1973), 1–34; "Horace's 'Ut Pictura Poesis': The Argument for Stylistic Decorum," *Traditio,* 34 (1978), 29–73.

On the principle of *oeconomia* see my *Hermeneutics and the Rhetorical Tradition,* 27–31.

giving just the right example to make his case. What, he asks, could be more absurd than "to start my explanation of the proverb An Iliad of troubles by proceeding to tell the whole history of the Trojan war, beginning (as Horace puts it) 'from that twin egg,' or to illustrate An invention worthy of Ulysses by unfolding the whole narrative of the *Odyssey?*" (LB, II, 713B; *CWE,* 34, 176; cf. *Ars Poetica* 147).

Erasmus even claims to be following decorum in avoiding the Horatian *callida iunctura,* the so-called clever connection or juxtaposition (*Ars Poetica* 47–48, 242). In a work such as the *Adages,* he argues, "it seemed to me somehow right and proper that there should be no order" (LB, II, 713DE; *CWE,* 34, 177). Not only would it weary the reader in so extended a work, but polishing it would have delayed publication the full Horatian nine years (LB, II, 713EF; *CWE,* 34, 177; *Ars Poetica* 388, and cf. 291).

Then distancing himself one final step from the artistic enterprise theorized in the *Ars,* Erasmus proclaims a communal, in contrast to a private, agenda—the Christian in contrast to the Roman way. For the Horatian poet who is truly accomplished effects the difficult task of making what is common his own private property (*Difficile est proprie communia dicere* [*Ars Poetica* 128]); or, as Horace continues, he wins private rights (*privatus ius*) to public property (*publica materies*) (*Ars Poetica* 131). The author of the *Adages,* in contrast, welcomes (so he says) the prospect of both shared labor and shared credit (LB, II, 715E; *CWE,* 34, 180). What holds for the writer seeking glory for himself, in other words, does not hold for the one who aims at being useful to the community (LB, II, 715C; *CWE,* 34, 179–80).[24] So Eras-

24. Although Horace imagines art (*ars*) and natural talent (*natura, ingenium*) sharing their wealth (*opes*) and property (*res*) in friendly (*amice*)—perhaps Pythagorean—style (410–11; cf. 167), he nevertheless expects the poet to make the *res* of literary tradition, also called the wealth

mus concludes the 1508 version of this adage by upholding the "general advantage (*publicum negocium*) of all who wish to learn" over "my own private ends" (*privatim*) (LB, II, 716B; *CWE*, 34, 181):

> But in my opinion at any rate, in rebuilding the re-public of letters (*res literaria*) one must display the spirit of a second Hercules, and no fear or weariness at the prospect of your own loss should discourage you from serving the common good.

Advancing the theme of the initial adage of the first and second thousands, the opening adage of the third thousand features the Aldine *Adages* as common intellectual property. In this more traditional sense, *res literaria* parallels *res publica;* the republic of letters—the common literary wealth—models itself on the political republic or commonwealth, whose paradigm, in turn, is the community of friends. In spite of the emerging legal sense of *res literaria* as *supellex literaria*—that is, literary property, on the model of material property, as privately owned and protected by law—Erasmus insists on the commonalities between liter-ary production and political practice: *studium* still imitating *im-perium*.

As we have seen, the very first of the more than three thou-sand adages—"Amicorum communia omnia"—sets in relief the intellectual communalism of the readers of the *Adages*. In the wake of its publication, all of them share equally the literary

---

or *opes* (307), his own private property (128–52). See C. O. Brink, *Horace on Poetry* (Cambridge, 1971), 204–07, 208–10, 432–42, 486–90. On the "friendship" between the poet and the critic, see Brink, 513–15.

Indeed, throughout the *Ars Poetica* Horace, like Roman law itself, places the emphasis on *res*. On the tripartite division of Roman law into *res, persona* and *actio,* with the greatest attention to matters of *res* or property, see above, p. 79.

wealth of antiquity. As we have also seen, "Festina lente" opens the second thousand by featuring the scholar-publisher as heir to antiquity and thus responsible for handing down the fully restored legacy of its literary tradition. In company with these two adages, as it were, "Herculei labores" introduces the third and last thousand of the Aldine edition by foregrounding the community-mindedness of the author-editor. Fully expecting the collaboration of other author-editors on this project (LB, II, 715E; *CWE*, 34, 180), he succeeds in making the *Adages* not only a common treasury of the intellectual wealth of so-called classical antiquity but also, toying with the emerging legal sense, a commonly held literary property. Despite his protestations in this adage against Horatian law, then, Erasmus has carefully arranged his work, effecting a more subtly decorous *callida iunctura:* not, to be sure, adage by adage, but rather thousand by thousand. Each succeeding *chilias* of the Aldine *Adagiorum chiliades* is introduced by an adage that returns the reader's attention to the question of property: not only to the newly published book she is reading as an article of material property but also and maybe even more significantly to the complex issues of ownership that attach to the intellectual property therein.

Conclusion

Looking back in 1523 on an *Adages* now in the prime of life, Erasmus, as we saw in the introduction, recalled for his friend Botzheim its birth and gradual development.[1] As we have just seen in the preceding chapter, the earliest phase of this development from the 1500 *Collectanea* to the Aldine *Adages* of 1508 was far from haphazard. Erasmus, we learned, used a chiliastic organization to draw his readers' attention to the deeply embedded but shifting issues of property that form the substrate of an apparently disorganized collection.[2] By tradition, as we also learned, these issues are linked with notions of friendship; and rooted in the deepest layer of this tradition is the adage Erasmus moves to first position to serve as introduction to the collection as a whole: "Friends hold all things in common."

Like the 1508 Aldine *Adages*, the 1515 Froben edition not only reaffirms the focus of the opening adage on friendship and property but does so once again by deftly marking the beginning of a new thousand. Standing at the head of the fourth *chilias* is the unusually long exposition of a newly added adage that Erasmus himself characterizes as both elegant (*elegans*) and well-known

---

1. On the growth of the *Adages* see Margaret Mann Phillips, 96–134.

2. For Erasmus' own characterization of the shape of his Aldine *Adages* see Ep. 211, Allen, I, 445; *CWE*, 2, 142, where he explains that "Instead of a consecutive order (if indeed there can be any kind of order in these matters), I substituted an index, in which I arranged by families those proverbs that seemed to be of the same stamp and to be related."

(*celebratum*): "Dulce bellum inexpertis"—"War is sweet to those who have not tried it" (LB, II, 951A–970E; Phillips, 308–53).[3] And Erasmus begins this lengthy essay by portraying war as the very antithesis of friendship. For humans were born, he argues, not for *bellum* but for *amicitia* (LB, II, 952AB; Phillips, 310)— an argument he supports by rewriting the etiological myth from the *Protagoras* concerning the origins of political life.

In the Platonic original of this myth, Protagoras both includes the art of war in the art of politics (*Protagoras* 321B) and singles out justice or *dikē* as the special ingredient in the mixture that is man (322D). The Erasmian version, in contrast, makes both a virtue of our deficiency (by imagining an Epimetheus who intentionally fashions us for concord instead of one who neglects to outfit us for conflict) and friendship the special seasoning (LB, II, 952C; Phillips, 311):[4]

> Only man was produced naked, weak, tender, un-
> armed, with very soft flesh and smooth skin. Among
> his members nothing would seem to have been in-
> tended for fighting and violence. . . . so that from
> this one may conjecture that this animal alone was
> born for friendship, which is initiated and cemented
> by mutual aid.

Armed only with a friendly eye and a friendly voice (LB, II, 952D; Phillips, 311), humans need above all else one another as friends (LB, II, 952EF; Phillips, 312). And whereas ancient philosophers, including Aristotle and Cicero, teach us that friend-

---

3. See Phillips, 298–300.
4. On the positive role of Epimetheus and its possible origins in Pythagoreanism see Michael J. B. Allen, *Synoptic Art: Marsilio Ficino on the History of Platonic Interpretation* (Florence, 1998), 157–58.

ship is the firmest foundation of political community, Erasmus adds in his exposition of this adage that more lasting than mere political partnership is the partnership rooted in shared intellectual pursuits—what he calls here a *societas honestorum studiorum* (LB, II, 952F; Phillips, 312).

Like the other adages in the forefront of their thousands, in other words, "Dulce bellum inexpertis" also effects the transfer from *imperium* to *studium*. Indeed, empire in this adage is far from the fruit of friendship; it is rather the engine of war. And more often than not, Erasmus insists, war is fought over ridiculous claims—*inanissimi tituli* (954B)—to some piece of property.

Fighting their private quarrels in the public arena, the European monarchs of Erasmus' day are so preoccupied with acquiring property that they confuse *imperium* with *dominium*—governorship with ownership (LB, II, 965AB; Phillips, 340–41):

> for the sake of asserting the right of dominion over one small town, they gravely imperil their whole realm (*imperium*). . . . I will only say this: if a claim to possession (*titulus*) is to be reckoned sufficient reason for going to war, then in such a disturbed state of human affairs, so full of change, there is no one who does not possess such a claim (*titulus*). What people has not, at one time or another been driven out of its lands. . . . How often has there been a transfer of sovereignty (*translata imperia*), either by chance or by treaty?

Adding to this confusion of claims, moreover, is the confusion of terms. For both the rulers and the ruled, mistakenly calling dominion or *dominium* what should more accurately be called administration or *administratio*, run the risk of confounding what can be owned with what cannot: an open field (*privatum agrum*) with a state (*civitas*), a herd of cattle with human beings (LB, II,

965C; Phillips, 341; cf. "Sileni Alcibiadis," LB, II, 775D; *CWE*, 34, 270).

Fully expecting his most hard-headed readers to reject both philosophy and philology, Erasmus saves his most pragmatic argument for last, making it, as his favorite philosopher often did, with the help of a story. Not incidentally, this story is about a quarrel over inheriting some property. In this particular case, two disputants, who happen to be kinsmen (*cognati*), reconcile when one persuades the other that they will not only both suffer financial loss from pressing their individual claims—a course of action that benefits only those paid to operate the legal machinery—but they will both also be much the poorer for the loss of their friendship. "Why don't we have an understanding between ourselves," the one asks the other (LB, II, 965F–966A; Phillips, 342):

> not with these knaves, and share out between us
> what we should have to pay out uselessly to them?
> You give up half yours, and I will give up half mine.
> In this way we shall be the richer for our friend-
> ship, which we were going otherwise to lose, and we
> shall escape a great deal of trouble. If you refuse to
> give up anything, I will leave the whole business for
> you to arrange. I would rather this money went to a
> friend than to those insatiable blood-suckers. It will
> be a great gain to me to have preserved my fair fame,
> kept a friend, and avoided such a mass of troubles.

Here, as we have already seen above in another cautionary tale about property, the half is more than the whole. Consequently, the cleverer of the two kinsmen, like this particular adage as well as the author of the essay glossing it, advocates peace over war, especially when the quarrel concerns property. Whereas war transforms private property disputes between kings into public pain and suffering, peace between nations engenders friendship among many (LB, II, 957D; Phillips, 322).

Like several of the most popular adages earlier in the collection, then, this one features friendship and property. As we have seen in previous chapters, Erasmus applauds Pythagoras and Plato throughout the *Adages* for their like-mindedness with Christ on the special link between these two key elements. All three philosophers insist on the commonality of friendship as the paradigm for ownership. In keeping with this like-mindedness, Erasmus invokes Pythagoras twice in this adage for his wisdom in rejecting any custom encouraging bellicose conduct (LB, II, 955C, 956D). As we have also seen in previous chapters, other ancient philosophers endorse friendship without extending its commonality to material property. In this adage, Erasmus censures Aristotle for making just this exception (LB, II, 961AB; Phillips, 331):

> From [Aristotle] we have learnt that human felicity cannot be complete without worldly goods—physical or financial. From him we have learnt that a state cannot flourish where all things are held in common. We try to combine all his doctrines with the teaching of Christ, which is like mixing water and fire.

Here noting the incompatibility between Christianity and Aristotelian philosophy, Erasmus invokes the debate, outlined in chapter 4, between the *Republic* and *Politics* on the issue of private ownership. And he follows this invocation with a rejection of Roman law. Even more than Aristotle's political philosophy, as we have seen in chapter 4, Roman law is grounded in private property—a grounding that tempers even Cicero's Platonizing. This adage, therefore, dismisses Roman law along with Aristotelian philosophy. Erasmus cannot sanction either a "just war" or the legal but immoderate accumulation of private goods (LB, II, 961BC; Phillips, 331).[5]

In describing for Botzheim the gradual expansion of his *Adages*, Erasmus no doubt has in mind the addition of new adages, like "Dulce bellum inexpertis"; he also has in mind the revision of previously included adages, like the 1515 version of

5. Like Erasmus, Budé, preeminent among the humanists as a legal scholar, notes not only the affinities between Pythagoras and Christ but the philosophical differences between Roman law and Christianity. See, for instance, Budé's letter to Thomas Lupset appended to the 1518 *Utopia* in *The Complete Works of St. Thomas More*, ed. Edward Surtz and J. H. Hexter (New Haven, 1965), IV, 9–10: "This happens, of course, in those generations, those institutions, those customs, in those nations which have pronounced it lawful that every man should have reputation and power in proportion to the resources by which he has built up his own family fortunes—he and his heirs. This process snowballs as great-great-greatgrandchildren and their great-great-grandchildren vie in increasing by splendid additions the patrimonies received from their forefathers— which amounts to saying that it snowballs as they oust, far and wide, their neighbors, their kindred by marriage, their relations by blood, and even their brothers and sisters. Yet Christ, the founder and supervisor of possessions, let among His followers a Pythagorean communion and charity (*Pythagoricam communionem & charitatem*) ratified by significant example when Ananias was condemned to death for breaking the law of communion. Certainly, by this arrangement, Christ seems to me to have abolished, among His own at least, the whole arrangement set up by the civil and canonical law of fairly recent date in contentious volumes. This law we see today holding the highest position in jurisprudence and controlling our destinies." And like Erasmus, Budé exploits the applicability of our Pythagorean adage. So he proposes, in a letter to Erasmus (Ep. 493, Allen, II, 402; *CWE*, 4, 151): "to form a partnership with you, if you concur, in all our friends, the more readily as you have already acquired a title not only to my friends but to myself, so that from now on there is a legal agreement between us for friendship of no ordinary kind expressed in these words in all good faith; and let us enter into this covenant on the understanding that we shall hold all our possessions in common and share our friends."

"Herculei labores." Whereas the earlier Aldine version of this adage ended, as we saw in the previous chapter, with Erasmus calling for cooperation on subsequent editions of this common literary property, this version ends with Erasmus claiming that his own heroism in the undertaking surpasses that of the ancient hero. For while Hercules himself proved unable to handle more than one task at a time, Erasmus, by his own account, successfully completed two Herculean labors at once—the new Froben *Adages*, to which this revision belongs, and Jerome's *Letters* (LB, II, 716C; *CWE*, 34, 181):

> For in Basel were being printed at the same moment both the Adagiorum Chiliades, so much corrected and enriched (*locupletataeque*) that the revision cost me no less than the earlier edition which I completed in Venice in the house of Aldus Manutius, and the complete works of St. Jerome, of which I had taken on my own shoulders the largest and almost most difficult part, the books of his *Letters*— no light task, in the Muses' name, even if one only had to read so many volumes.

Echoing the letter to Botzheim in its characterization of the *Adages* as a repository or treasury enriched (*locupletata*) over time, this addition also draws our attention to another literary property in which Erasmus claims some proprietary right.

In the dedicatory letter to William Warham, Archbishop of Canterbury, introducing the edition of Jerome's *Letters* that forms part of the Froben *Opera omnia* in nine volumes (1516), Erasmus substantiates this claim.[6] Here as elsewhere, he begins

6. In the letter to Botzheim (Allen, I, 42; *CWE*, 24, 697), Erasmus lists the edition of Jerome's letters among his own works. For a discussion of the dedicatory letter to Warham, see Jardine, 164.

by subordinating *imperium* to *studium* and reflects on the complex nature of the property that makes such intellectual activity possible. On the one hand, as we have already learned in "Festina lente," rulers themselves consider the accumulation of riches contained in their imperial libraries among their most treasured possessions (Allen, II, 212; *CWE*, 3, 255):

> This was, they thought, the way to secure the truest and most lasting renown for themselves and a special ornament for their kingdoms, if they bequeathed (*traderent*) to posterity a library equipped with most accurate copies of the very best authors; nor did they think a more serious loss could befall them than the destruction of any of their riches in this kind.

On the other hand, Erasmus laments here as in "Dulce bellum," these same rulers often risk all their wealth to acquire a paltry piece of land. How much more justifiable is the expenditure of so much labor on recovering really valuable property, like Jerome's writings, from damage and loss. Indeed, whoever possesses these writings—and here Erasmus clearly has in mind more than the material book—possesses real wealth (Allen, II, 220; *CWE*, 3, 265):

> It is a river of gold, a well-stocked library (*locupletissimam bibliothecam*), that a man acquires who possesses Jerome and nothing else. He does not possess him, on the other hand, if his text is like what used to be in circulation, all confusion and impurity.

While more concerned with intellectual than material property, however, Erasmus nevertheless emphasizes that only by using his edition, whose purification cost the editor so much labor, does the reader acquire Jerome and no one else.

By careful, corrected, and meditative reading, Erasmus affirms, one eventually makes Jerome or whatever else one reads one's own. In his own case, however, Erasmus' exploitation of the legal language of ownership makes a double point. For Erasmus claims not only to have read Jerome with the care of one who meditates but also to feel entitled to the *Letters* as his own literary property on the grounds of long possession and use—and maybe even, recalling the usual justification for privilege, as the rightful fruits of his own much-recorded labor (Allen, II, 220; *CWE*, 3, 265):[7]

> I have done what bankrupts often do. . . . Or rather, to compare a situation even more like mine, I have followed the example of those who would rather raise a fresh loan than go to prison for non-payment, and have borrowed from Jerome the wherewithal to repay you. Though why should it any longer look like something borrowed rather than my own?— real estate (*multae res soli*) often passes from one ownership to another by occupation or prescriptive right (*occupatione vel praescriptione*). In any case, in this line of business Jerome himself has laid down a principle for me in his preface to the books of Kings, repeatedly calling that work his, because anything that we have made our own by correcting, reading, constant devotion, we can fairly claim is ours (*id iure nobis vindicamus*). On this principle why should not I myself claim a proprietary right in the works of Jerome (*Hac lege cur non et ipse mihi ius vindicem in*

7. Together, the 1508 and 1515 endings echo the two arguments used to justify the granting of privileges: the fruits of an individual's labors and the interest of the community.

Hieronymianis libris)? For centuries they had been treated as abandoned goods; I entered upon them as something ownerless, and by incalculable efforts reclaimed them for all devotees of the true theology.

In putting these rhetorical questions to Warham in such boldly legal terms, Erasmus predicts the collision between two kinds of profit: one is the kind heirs of an intellectual tradition like the one stored in the *Adages* have expected for centuries from their investment in the works of the past; the other is the kind that comes increasingly to be expected by purveyors of literary property.

Momentarily looking ahead to the battles over commercial profits tied to the printing industry, Erasmus nevertheless couches this forward glance in his customary strategy of looking back. Jerome himself, Erasmus contends, authorizes the editor's claim to the abandoned literary property he restores. For the time being, then, Erasmus uses the traditional form of the dedicatory epistle to put the case rhetorically. In due time, as students of the early history of copyright know, others will press their claims more juridically in courts of law. In the meantime, some of Erasmus' own most thoughtful readers, inheriting with his help a vastly enriched ancient literary tradition, will deploy its weapons in their own struggles for "the just retaining of each man his several copy."[8]

8. John Milton, *Areopagitica* in *Complete Poems and Major Prose*, ed. Merritt Y. Hughes (Indianapolis, 1957), 749. On the early history of copyright, see above, ch. 6, n. 6. And see Rose, *Authors and Owners*, esp. 28–30.

Bibliography of Secondary Sources

Amand, David. *L'Ascèse Monastique de Saint Basile.* Louvain, 1948.

Annas, Julia. "Cicero on Stoic Moral Philosophy and Private Property." In *Philosophia Togata: Essays on Philosophy and Roman Society,* edited by Miriam Griffin and Jonathan Barnes. Oxford, 1989.

Appelt, Theodore Charles. *Studies in the Contents and Sources of Erasmus' "Adagia."* Chicago, 1942.

Arendt, Hannah. *The Human Condition.* Chicago, 1958; rpt. 1989.

Armstrong, Elizabeth. *Before Copyright: The French Book Privilege System, 1498–1526.* Cambridge, 1990.

Arnold, Diane W. H., and Pamela Bright, eds. *De doctrina christiana: A Classic of Western Culture.* Notre Dame, 1995.

Atkins, E. M. " 'Domina et Regina Virtutum': Justice and Societas in *De Officiis.*" *Phronesis* 35 (1990): 258–89.

Augustijn, Cornelis. *Erasmus: His Life, Works, and Influence.* Translated by J. C. Grayson. Toronto, 1991.

Bainton, Roland H. *Erasmus of Christendom.* New York, 1969; rpt. 1982.

Barker, Ernest. *The Political Thought of Plato and Aristotle.* New York, 1959.

Barnes, Timothy. *Tertullian.* Oxford, 1971.

Barnett, Mary Jane. "Erasmus and the Hermeneutics of Linguistic Praxis." *Renaissance Quarterly* 49 (1996): 542–72.

Bateman, John J. "From Soul to Soul: Persuasion in Erasmus' Paraphrases on the New Testament." *Erasmus in English* 15 (1987/1988): 7–16.

Benardete, Seth. *The Rhetoric of Morality and Philosophy: Plato's "Gorgias" and "Phaedrus."* Chicago, 1991.

————. *Socrates' Second Sailing: On Plato's "Republic."* Chicago, 1989.

Berger, Harry, Jr. "*Phaedrus* and the Politics of Inscription." In *Plato and Postmodernism,* edited by Steven Shankman. Glenside, Penn., 1994.

Bietenholz, Peter G. "Ethics and Early Printing: Erasmus' Rules for the Proper Conduct of Authors." *Humanities Association Review* 26 (1975): 180–95.

Boyancé, Pierre. "Sur la vie pythagoricienne." *Revue des Etudes Grecques* 52 (1939): 36–50.

Boyle, Marjorie O'Rourke. *Christening Pagan Mysteries: Erasmus in Pursuit of Wisdom.* Toronto, 1981.

Brakke, David. *Athanasius and the Politics of Asceticism.* Oxford, 1995.

Brink, C. O. *Horace on Poetry.* Cambridge, 1971.

———. *Horace on Poetry: Prolegomena to the Literary Epistles.* Cambridge, 1963.

Brockwell, C. W. "Augustine's Ideal Monastic Community: A Paradigm for the Doctrine of the Church." *Augustinian Studies* 8 (1977): 91–109.

Bromley, Marilynne. "Erasmus *ΣΠΟΥΔΟΓΕΛΟΙΟΣ*: Colloquia and Satura." *Classical and Modern Literature* 7 (1987): 295–307.

Brown, Cynthia J. "Text, Image, and Authorial Self-Consciousness in Late Medieval Paris." In *Printing the Written Word: The Social History of Books, c. 1450–1520*, edited by Sandra Hindman. (Ithaca, 1991).

Brown, Peter. *The Making of Late Antiquity.* Cambridge, Mass., 1978; rpt. 1998.

———. *Power and Persuasion in Late Antiquity: Towards a Christian Empire.* Madison, Wisc., 1992.

Brunt, P. A. " 'Amicitia' in the Late Roman Republic." *Proceedings of the Cambridge Philological Society,* n.s., 11 (1965): 1–20.

Buck, Günther. "The Structure of Hermeneutic Experience and the Problem of Tradition." *New Literary History* 10 (1978): 31–47.

Buckland, W. W. *A Text-Book of Roman Law from Augustus to Justinian.* Cambridge, 1921.

Burkert, Walter. *Lore and Science in Ancient Pythagoreanism.* Translated by Edwin L. Minor, Jr. Cambridge, Mass., 1972.

Callahan, Virginia W. "The Erasmus-Hercules Equation in the Emblems of Alciati." In *The Verbal and the Visual: Essays in Honor of William Sebastian Heckscher,* edited by Karl-Ludwig Selig and Elizabeth Sears. New York, 1990.

Camargo, Martin. " 'Non solum sibi sed aliis etiam': Neoplatonism and Rhetoric in Saint Augustine's *De doctrina christiana.*" *Rhetorica* 16 (1998): 393–408.

Campion, Edmund. "Defenses of Classical Learning in St. Augustine's *De Doctrina Christiana* and Erasmus' *Antibarbari.*" *History of European Ideas* 4 (1983): 467–72.

Carter, L. B. *The Quiet Athenian.* Oxford, 1986.

Celenza, Christopher S. "Pythagoras in the Renaissance: The Case of Marsilio Ficino." *Renaissance Quarterly* 52 (1999): 667–711.

Chartier, Roger, and Daniel Roche. "New Approaches to the History of the Book." In *Constructing the Past. Essays in Historical Methodology*, edited by Jacques Le Goff and Pierre Nora. Cambridge, 1985.

Chavasse, Ruth. "The First Known Author's Copyright, September 1486, in the Context of a Humanist Career." *Bulletin of the John Rylands University Library of Manchester* 69 (1986): 11–37.

Chomarat, Jacques, ed. *Actes du Colloque International Erasme.* Geneva, 1990.

——. *Grammaire et Rhétorique chez Erasme,* 2 vols. Paris, 1981.

Christian, L. G. "The Figure of Socrates in Erasmus' Works." *Sixteenth-Century Journal* 3 (1972): 1–10.

Clark, Elizabeth A. *The Origenist Controversy: The Cultural Construction of an Early Christian Debate.* Princeton, 1992.

Cohen, David. "Law, Autonomy, and Political Community in Plato's *Laws*." *Classical Philology* 88 (1993): 301–17.

——. *Law, Sexuality and Society: The Enforcement of Morals in Classical Athens.* Cambridge, 1991.

Coleman, Joyce. *Public Reading and the Reading Public in Late Medieval England and France.* Cambridge, 1996.

Coleman, Robert. "The Dream of Cicero." *Proceedings of the Cambridge Philological Society,* n.s., 10 (1964): 1–14.

Compagnon, Antoine. *La seconde main: ou le travail de la citation.* Paris, 1979.

Congar, Yves M.-J. *Tradition and Traditions.* New York, 1967.

Coogan, Robert. "The Pharisee against the Hellenist: Edward Lee versus Erasmus." *Renaissance Quarterly* 39 (1986): 476–506.

Cooper, John M. "Aristotle on Friendship." In *Essays on Aristotle's Ethics*, edited by Amélie Oksenberg Rorty. Berkeley, 1980.

Costa, Dennis. "Domesticating the Divine Economy: Humanist Theology in Erasmus' *Convivia*." In *Creative Imitation: New Essays on Renaissance Literature in Honor of Thomas M. Greene,* edited by David Quint, Margaret W. Ferguson, J. W. Pigman III and Wayne A. Rebhorn. *Medieval and Renaissance Texts and Studies.* Binghamton, 1992.

Cox, P. *Biography in Late Antiquity: The Quest for the Holy Man.* Berkeley, 1983.

Cytowska, Maria. "Erasme de Rotterdam et Marsile Ficin son maître." *Eos* 63 (1975): 165–79.

——. "Erasme de Rotterdam, Traducteur d'Homère." *Eos* 63 (1975): 341–53.

Darnton, Robert. "First Steps Toward a History of Reading." In *The Kiss of Lamourette: Reflections in Cultural History*. New York, 1990.

———. "What is the History of Books?" In *The Kiss of Lamourette: Reflections in Cultural History*. New York, 1990.

Davis, Natalie Zemon. "Beyond the Market: Books as Gifts in Sixteenth-Century France." *Transactions of the Royal Historical Society* 33 (1983): 69–88.

———. "Proverbial Wisdom and Popular Errors." In *Society and Culture in Early Modern France*. Stanford, 1975.

de Lubac, Henri. *Exégèse Médiévale: Les Quatre Sens de l'Ecriture*. 2 vols. Paris, 1959.

De Vogel, C. J. *Pythagoras and Early Pythagoreanism*. Assen, 1966.

de Vries, G. J. *A Commentary on the Phaedrus of Plato*. Amsterdam, 1969.

Dillon, John M. " 'Orthodoxy' and 'Eclecticism': Middle Platonists and Neo-Pythagoreans." In *The Question of "Eclecticism": Studies in Later Greek Philosophy*. Berkeley, 1988.

Dunn, Kevin. "Milton among the monopolists: *Areopagitica*, Intellectual Property and the Hartlib Circle." In *Samuel Hartlib and Universal Reformation: Studies in Intellectual Communication*, edited by Mark Greengrass, Michael Leslie, and Timothy Raylor. Cambridge, 1994.

Eden, Kathy. " 'Between Friends All is Common': The Erasmian Adage and Tradition." *Journal of the History of Ideas* 59 (1998): 405–19.

———. *Hermeneutics and the Rhetorical Tradition: Chapters in the Ancient Legacy and Its Humanist Reception*. New Haven, 1997.

———. "*Koinonia* and the Friendship between Rhetoric and Religion." In *Rhetorical Invention and Religious Inquiry*, edited by W. Jost and W. Olmsted. New Haven, 2000.

———. *Poetic and Legal Fiction in the Aristotelian Tradition*. Princeton, 1986.

Edwards, Mark J. "Two Images of Pythagoras: Iamblichus and Porphyry." In *The Divine Iamblichus: Philosopher and Man of Gods*, edited by H. J. Blumenthal and E. G. Clark. London, 1993.

Else, Gerald F. *The Structure and Date of Book 10 of Plato's "Republic."* Heidelberg, 1972.

Feather, John. "From rights in copies to copyright: the recognition of authors' rights in English law and practice in the sixteenth and seventeenth centuries." *Cardozo Arts and Entertainment Law Journal* 10 (1992): 455–73.

Ferrari, G. R. F. *Listening to the Cicadas: A Study of Plato's "Phaedrus."* Cambridge, 1987.

Ferrary, Jean-Louis. "The Statesman and the Law in the Political Philosophy of Cicero." In *Justice and Generosity: Studies in Hellenistic Social
and Political Philosophy.* Cambridge, 1995.

Festugière, André-Jean. *Personal Religion Among the Greeks.* Berkeley,
1954.

Finley, M. I., ed. *Studies in Roman Property.* Cambridge, 1976.

Florovsky, Georges. "The Function of Tradition in the Ancient Church."
The Greek Orthodox Theological Review 9 (1963/1964): 181–200.

Foley, Helene P. "'The Mother of the Argument': Eros and the Body in
Sappho and Plato's *Phaedrus.*" In *Parchments of Gender: Deciphering the
Bodies of Antiquity,* edited by Maria Wyke. Oxford, 1998.

Fraisse, Jean-Claude. *Philia: La Notion d'amitié dans la philosophie anitque.*
Paris, 1974.

Friedlaender, Paul. *Plato.* 3 vols. Princeton, 1969.

Friesen, Abraham. *Erasmus, the Anabaptists, and the Great Commission.*
Grand Rapids, 1998.

Fulin, R. "Documenti per servire alla storia della tipografia veneziana."
Archivio veneto 23 (1882): 84–212.

———. "Primi privilegi di stampa in Venezia." *Archivio veneto* 1 (1871):
160–64.

Fumaroli, Marc. *Dix Conférences sur Erasme: Eloge de la Folie et Colloques,*
ed. Léon-E. Halkin. Paris, 1988.

Gadamer, Hans-Georg. "Plato and the Poets." In *Dialogue and Dialectic.*
Translated by P. Christopher Smith. New Haven, 1980.

Geanakoplos, Deno John. *Greek Scholars in Venice: Studies in the Dissemi-
nation of Greek Learning from Byzantium to Western Europe.* Cambridge,
Mass., 1962.

Godin, André. "The Enchiridion Militis Christiani: The Modes of an
Origenian Appropriation." *Erasmus of Rotterdam Society Yearbook* 2
(1982): 47–79.

———. *Erasme Lecteur D'Origène.* Geneva, 1982.

Gottfried, Bruce. "Pan, the Cicadas, and Plato's Use of Myth in the
Phaedus." In *Plato's Dialogues: New Studies and Interpretations,* edited
by Gerald A. Press. Lanham, Md., 1993.

Gould, Thomas. *The Ancient Quarrel Between Poetry and Philosophy.*
Princeton, 1990.

Grafton, Anthony. *Commerce with the Classics: Ancient Books and Renaissance Readers.* Ann Arbor, 1997.

———. "Correctores corruptores? Notes on the Social History of Editing." In *Editing Texts: Texte Edieren,* edited by Glenn W. Most. Göttingen, 1998.

Grafton, Anthony, and Lisa Jardine. *From Humanism to the Humanities.* Cambridge, Mass., 1986.

Greech, Prosper. "The Augustinian Community and Primitive Church." *Augustiniana* 5 (1955): 459–70.

Greene, Thomas M. "Erasmus' 'Festina Lente': Vulnerabilities of the Humanist Text." In *Mimesis, From Mirror to Method: Augustine to Descartes,* edited by John D. Lyons and Stephen G. Nichols, Jr. Hanover, 1982.

———. *The Vulnerable Text: Essays on Renaissance Literature.* New York, 1986.

Gerlin, Andrea. "Community and Ascesis: Paul's Directives to the Corinthians Interpreted in the *Rule* of Augustine." In *Collectanea Augustiniana.* New York, 1990.

Goehring, James E. "The Origins of Monasticism." In *Eusebius, Christianity, and Judaism,* edited by H. W. Aldridge and G. Hata. Detroit, 1992.

Greer, Rowan. *Broken Lights and Mended Lives: Theology and Common Life in the Early Church.* University Park, Penn., 1986.

Gregg, Robert C. *Consolation Philosophy: Greek and Christian "Paideia" in Basil and the Two Gregories.* Cambridge, Mass., 1975.

Grendler, Paul. "Printing and Censorship." In *The Cambridge History of Renaissance Philosophy,* edited by C. B. Schmitt et al. Cambridge, 1988.

Griswold, Charles L. "Gadamer and the Interpretation of Plato." *Ancient Philosophy* 1,2 (1981): 171–78.

———. *Self-Knowledge in Plato's Phaedrus.* New Haven, 1986.

Gueguen, John A. "Reading More's *Utopia* as a Criticism of Plato." In *Quincentennial Essays on St. Thomas More,* edited by Michael J. Moore. Boone, North Carolina, 1978.

Guzie, T. W. "Patristic Hermeneutics and the Meaning of Tradition." *Theological Studies* 32 (1971): 647–58.

Habinek, Thomas N. "Towards a History of Friendly Advice: The Politics of Candor in Cicero's *de Amicitia.*" *Apeiron* 23 (1990): 165–85.

Hadas, Moses, and Morton Smith. *Heroes and Gods: Spiritual Biographies in Antiquity.* New York, 1962.

Hadot, Pierre. *Philosophy as a Way of Life.* Translated by Michael Chase. Oxford, 1995.

Halliburton, R. J. "The Inclination to Retirement: The Retreat of Cassiciacum and the 'Monastery' of Tagaste." *Studia Patristica* 5 (1962): 329–40.

Hankins, James. *Plato in the Renaissance,* 2 vols. Leiden, 1990.

Hanson, R. P. C. *Origen's Doctrine of Tradition.* London, 1954.

Harrison, A. R. W. *The Law of Athens: The Family and Property.* Oxford, 1968.

Hendrickson, G. L. "Ancient Reading." *Classical Journal* 25 (1929/30): 182–96.

Heninger, S. K., Jr. "Pythagorean Symbola in Erasmus' *Adagia.*" *Renaissance Quarterly* 21 (1968): 162–65.

———. *Touches of Sweet Harmony: Pythagorean Cosmology and Renaissance Poetics.* San Marino, Calif., 1974.

Hindman, Sandra, ed. *Printing the Written Word: The Social History of Books, circa 1450–1520.* Ithaca, 1991.

Hirsch, Rudolf. *Printing, Selling and Reading 1450–1550.* Wiesbaden, 1967.

Hutter, Horst. *Politics as Friendship: The origins of classical notions of politics in the theory and practice of friendship.* Waterloo, Ontario, 1978.

Jardine, Lisa. *Erasmus, Man of Letters.* Princeton, 1993.

Jeanneret, Michel. *A Feast of Words: Banquets and Table Talk in the Renaissance.* Translated by Jeremy Whiteley and Emma Hughes. Chicago, 1991.

Johnson, Luke T. *Sharing Possessions.* Philadelphia, 1981.

Kahn, Charles H. "Proleptic Composition in the *Republic,* or Why Book I was Never a Separate Dialogue." *Classical Quarterly* 43 (1993): 131–42.

Kelley, Donald R. "Gaius Noster: Substructures of Western Social Thought." In *History, Law and the Human Sciences.* London, 1984.

Kinney, Daniel. "Erasmus' Adages: midwife to the rebirth of classical learning." *Journal of Medieval and Renaissance Studies* 11 (1981): 169–92.

Kohls, Ernst-Wilhelm. *Die Theologie des Erasmus.* 2 vols. Basel, 1966.

———. "The Principal Theological Thoughts in the *Enchiridion Militis Christiani.*" In *Essays on the Works of Erasmus,* edited by Richard De Molen. New Haven, 1978.

Konstan, David. "Friendship and the State: The Context of Cicero's *De Amicitia.*" *Hyperboreus* 1 (1994/1995): 1–16.

———. *Friendship in the Classical World.* Cambridge, 1997.

Kraye, Jill, ed. *The Cambridge Companion to Renaissance Humanism.* Cambridge, 1996.

Kustas, George L. "Saint Basil and the Rhetorical Tradition." In *Basil of Caesarea: Christian, Humanist, Ascetic,* edited by Paul J. Fedwick. Toronto, 1981.

Laks, André. "Legislation and Demiurgy: On the Relationship Between Plato's *Republic* and *Laws*." *Classical Antiquity* 9 (1990): 209–29.

Langer, Ullrich. *Perfect Friendship: Studies in Literature and Moral Philosophy from Boccaccio to Corneille.* Geneva, 1994.

Lanham, Carol Dana. "Freshman Composition in the Early Middle Ages: Epistolography and Rhetoric before the Ars Dictaminis." *Viator: Medieval and Renaissance Studies* 23 (1992): 115–34.

Larsen, Bent Dalsgaard. *Jamblique de Chalcis: Exégète et Philosophe.* Aarhus, 1972.

Lawless, George. *Augustine of Hippo and his Monastic Rule.* Oxford, 1987.

Le Clercq, Jean. *Etudes sur le Vocabulaire Monastique du Moyen Age.* Rome, 1961.

———. *The Love of Learning and the Desire for God.* Translated by Catharine Misrahi. New York, 1982.

———. "Pour l'histoire de l'expression 'philosophe chrétienne'." *Mélange de Science Religieuse* 9 (1952): 221–26.

Lienhard, Joseph T. *Paulinus of Nola and Early Western Monasticism.* Cologne, 1977.

Long, A. A. "Cicero's Plato and Aristotle." In *Cicero the Philosopher,* edited by J. G. F. Powell. Oxford, 1995.

———. "Cicero's Politics in *De Officiis.*" In *Justice and Generosity: Studies in Hellenistic Social and Political Philosophy,* edited by André Laks and Malcolm Schofield. Cambridge, 1995.

Lowry, Martin. *Nicholas Jenson and the Rise of Venetian Publishing in Renaissance Europe.* Oxford, 1991.

———. *The World of Aldus Manutius: Business and Scholarship in Renaissance Venice.* Ithaca, New York, 1979.

MacDowell, Douglas M. *The Law in Classical Athens.* London, 1978.

MacIntyre, A. "Epistemological Crises, Dramatic Narrative and the Philosophy of Science." *Monist* 60 (1977): 453–72.

Madec, Goulven. *Saint Augustin et la Philosophie.* Paris, 1996.

Maffei, Domenico. "Les Débuts de l'activité de Budé, Alciat et Zase ainsi que quelques remarques sur Aymer du Rivail." In *Pédagogues et Juristes,* edited by Pierre Mesnard. Paris, 1963.

Malingrey, Anne-Marie. *"Philosophia": Etude d'un groupe de mots dans la littérature grecque, des Présocratiques au IVe siècle après J.-C.* Paris, 1961.

Margolin, Jean-Claude. *Erasme: Précepteur de L'Europe.* Paris, 1995.

Markus, R. A. "De civitate dei: Pride and the Common Good." In *Collectanea Augustiniana,* edited by Joseph C. Schnaubelt and Frederick Van Fleteren. New York, 1990.

―――. *The End of Ancient Christianity*. Cambridge, 1990.

――― . "Vie Monastique et Ascétisme chez Saint Augustin." In *Congresso Internazionale su S. Agostino nel XVI Centenario della Conversione*. Rome, 1987.

McGrath, Alistair E. "Divine Justice and Divine Equity in the Controversy between Augustine and Julien of Eclanum." *Downside Review* 101 (1983): 312–19.

McGuire, Brian Patrick. *Friendship and Community: The Monastic Experience*. Kalamazoo, 1988.

MacNamara, Marie Aquinas. *L'Amitié chez Saint Augustin*. Paris, 1961.

Malunowiczowna, Leokadia. "Le problème de l'amitié chez Basile, Grégoire de Nazianze, et Jean Chrysostome." *Studia Patristica* 16 (1985): 412–27.

Mathie, William. "Property in the Political Science of Aristotle." In *Theories of Property: Aristotle to the Present*, edited by Anthony Parel and Thomas Flanagan. Waterloo, Ontario, 1979.

Mealand, D. L. "Community of Goods and Utopian Allusions in Acts II-IV." *Journal of Theological Studies*, n.s., 28 (1977): 96–99.

Meeks, Wayne A. *The First Urban Christians: The Social World of the Apostle Paul*. New Haven, 1983.

Meredith, A. "Asceticism—Christian and Greek." *Journal of Theological Studies*, n.s., 27 (1976): 313–32.

Mesnard, Pierre. "Erasme et Budé." *Bulletin de l'Association Guillaume Budé* 4 (1965): 307–31.

Minar, Edwin L. "Pythagorean Communism." *Transactions and Proceedings of the American Philological Association* 75 (1944): 34–46.

Mitchell, Alan C. "The Social Function of Friendship in Acts 2:44–47 and 4:32–37." *Journal of Biblical Literature* 111 (1992): 255–72.

Morrison, J. S. "The Origins of Plato's Philosopher-Statesman." *Classical Quarterly*, n.s., 8 (1958): 198–218.

―――. "Pythagoras of Samos." *Classical Quarterly*, n.s., 6 (1956): 135–56.

Morrow, Glenn R. *Plato's Cretan City: A Historical Interpretation of the "Laws."* Princeton, 1960; rpt. 1993.

Natali, Carlo. "*Oikonomia* in Hellenistic Political Thought." In *Justice and Generosity*, edited by André Laks and Malcolm Schofield. Cambridge, 1995.

Nichols, Mary P. *Socrates and the Political Community*. Albany, 1987.

Nussbaum, Martha Craven. "Shame, Separateness, and Political Unity: Aristotle's Criticism of Plato." In *Essays on Aristotle's Ethics*, edited by Amélie Oksenberg Rorty. Berkeley, 1980.

Olin, John C. "Erasmus' *Adagia* and More's *Utopia*." In *Miscellanea Moreana: Essays for Germain Marc'hadour,* edited by Clare M. Murphy, Henri Gibaud, and Mario A. DiCesare. *Medieval & Renaissance Texts & Studies* 61 (1989): 127–36.

O'Meara, Dominic J. *Pythagoras Revived: Mathematics and Philosophy in Late Antiquity.* Oxford, 1989.

O'Sullivan, Neil. *Alcidamas, Aristophanes and the Beginnings of Greek Stylistic Theory.* Stuttgart, 1992.

Outler, Albert C. "The Sense of Tradition in the Ante-Nicene Church." In *The Heritage of Christian Thought: Essays in Honor of Robert Lowry Calhoun,* edited by Robert E. Cushman and Egil Grislis. New York, 1965.

Parel, Anthony and Thomas Flanagan, eds. *Theories of Property: Aristotle to the Present.* Waterloo, Ontario Canada, 1979.

Pfeiffer, Rudolf. *History of Classical Scholarship, 1300–1850.* Oxford, 1976.

Philip, J.A. *Pythagoras and Early Pythagoreanism.* Toronto, 1966.

Phillips, Margaret Mann. "Comment s'est on servi des Adages?" In *Actes du Colloque International Erasme,* edited by Jacques Chomarat, André Godin, and Jean-Claude Margolin. Geneva, 1990.

———. "La 'Philosophia Christi' reflétée dans les 'Adages' d'Erasme." In *Courants Religieux et Humanisme à la fin du XVe et au début du XVIe siècle.* Paris, 1959.

———. *The "Adages" of Erasmus.* Cambridge, 1964.

———. "Way with Adages." In *Essays on the Works of Erasmus,* edited by Richard L. DeMolen. New Haven, 1978.

Pollard, T. E. "The Exegesis of Scripture and the Arian Controversy." *The Collection of the John Ryland Library* 41 (1959): 414–29.

Prager, F. D. "The Early Growth and Influence of Intellectual Property." *Journal of the Patent Office Society* 34 (1952): 106–40.

Price, A. W. *Love and Friendship in Plato and Aristotle.* Oxford, 1986.

Quasten, Johannes. "A Pythagorean Idea in Jerome." *Ancient Journal of Philology* 63 (1942): 207–15.

———. "Tertullian and 'Tradition'." *Traditio* 2 (1944): 481–84.

Quillen, Carol E. "Plundering the Egyptians: Petrarch and Augustine's *De doctrina christiana.*" In *Reading and Wisdom: The De Doctrina Christiana of Augustine in the Middle Ages,* edited by Edward D. English. Notre Dame, 1995.

———. "A Tradition Invented: Petrarch, Augustine, and the Language of Humanism." *Journal of the History of Ideas* 53 (1992): 179–207.

Rabil, Albert, Jr. "Cicero and Erasmus' Moral Philosophy." *Erasmus of Rotterdam Society Yearbook* 8 (1988): 70-90

Rawson, Elizabeth. *Intellectual Life in the Late Roman Republic.* London, 1985.

Reese, Alan W. " 'So Outstanding an Athlete of Christ': Erasmus and the Significance of Jerome's Asceticism." *Erasmus of Rotterdam Society Yearbook* 8 (1998): 104-17.

Rice, Eugene F., Jr. "Erasmus and the Religious Tradition." *Journal of the History of Ideas* 11 (1950): 387-411.

———. *Saint Jerome in the Renaissance.* Baltimore, 1985.

Rist, John M. "Basil's 'Neoplatonism': Its Background and Nature." In *Basil of Caesarea: Christian, Humanist, Ascetic*, vol. 1, edited by Paul J. Fedwick. Toronto, 1981.

Robinson, A. J. K. "The Evolution of Copyright, 1476-1776." *The Cambrian Law Review* 22 (1991): 55-77.

Root, Robert K. "Publication Before Printing." *PMLA* 28 (1913): 417-31.

Rose, Mark. *Authors and Owners: The Invention of Copyright.* Cambridge, Mass., 1993.

———. "The author as proprietor: Donaldson v. Becket and the genealogy of modern authorship." *Representations* 23 (1988): 51-85.

Rosen, Edward. "Was Copernicus a Pythagorean?" *Isis* 53 (1962): 504-09.

Rosen, Stanley. "The Non-Lover in Plato's *Phaedrus*." In *Plato: True and Sophistic Rhetoric*, edited by Keith V. Erickson. Amsterdam, 1979.

Rousseau, Philip. *Basil of Caesarea.* Berkeley, 1994.

Rowe, C. J. "The Argument and Structure of Plato's *Phaedrus*." *Proceedings of the Cambridge Philological Society* n.s., 32 (1986).

Rummel, Erika. *Erasmus and his Catholic Critics.* 2 vols. Nieuwkoop, 1989.

———. *The Humanist-Scholastic Debate in the Renaissance and Reformation.* Cambridge, Mass., 1995.

———. "Quoting Poetry Instead of Scripture: Erasmus and Eucharius on *Contemptus Mundi*." *Bibliothèque d'Humanisme et Renaissance* 45 (1983): 503-09.

———. "The Reception of Erasmus' *Adages* in Sixteenth-Century England." *Renaissance and Reformation* 18 (1994): 19-30.

Russo, Joseph. "The Poetics of the Ancient Greek Proverb." *Journal of Folklore Research* 20 (1983): 121-30.

Santas, Gerasimos. "Passionate Platonic Love in the *Phaedrus*." *Ancient Philosophy* 2 (1982): 105-114.

Saulnier, V. L. "Proverbe et Paradoxe du XVe au XVIe Siècle." *Colloques internationaux du Centre national de la recherche scientifique* 15 (1950), 87–104.

Saunders, Trevor J. "The Property Classes and the Value of the *KΛΗΡΟΣ* in Plato's Laws," *Eranos* 58 (1961): 29–39.

———. "The Structure of the Soul and the State in Plato's Laws." *Eranos* 59 (1962): 37–55.

Schoeck, R. J. *Erasmus of Europe: The Prince of Humanists, 1501–1536.* Edinburgh, 1993.

Schofield, Malcolm. "Cicero's Definition of *Res Publica.*" In *Cicero the Philosopher,* edited by J. G. F. Powell. Oxford, 1995.

Shorey, Paul. "Plato's *Laws* and the Unity of Plato's Thought." *Classical Philology* 9 (1914): 345–69.

Schottenloher, Otto. "Erasme et la Respublica Christiana." In *Colloquia erasmiana turonensia,* edited by Jean-Claude Margolin. Toronto, 1972.

Schulz, Fritz. *Classical Roman Law.* Oxford, 1951.

Sharp, Ronald A. *Friendship and Literature: Spirit and Form.* Durham, 1986.

Sider, Robert D. " 'In Terms Quite Plain and Clear': The Exposition of Grace in the New Testament Paraphrases of Erasmus." *Erasmus in English* 15 (1987/1988): 16–25.

Smith, Preserved. *Erasmus: A Study of His Life, Ideals and Place in History.* New York: 1923; rpt. 1962.

———. *A Key to the Colloquies of Erasmus.* Cambridge, Mass., 1927.

Sorabji, Richard. *Animal Minds and Human Morals: The Origin of the Western Debate.* London, 1993.

Stalley, R. F. *An Introduction to Plato's Laws.* Oxford, 1983.

Strauss, Leo. *The Argument and the Action of Plato's Laws.* Chicago, 1975.

Stock, Brian. *Augustine the Reader: Meditation, Self-knowledge, and the Ethics of Interpretation.* Cambridge, Mass., 1996.

Swanson, Roy Arthur. "Ovid's Pythagorean Essay." *Classical Journal* 54 (1958): 21–24.

Thesleff, Holger. "An Introduction to the Pythagorean Writings of the Hellenistic Period." *Acta Academiae Aboensis* 24 (1961): 5–140.

———. "Okkelos, Archytas, and Plato." *Eranos* 59 (1962): 8–36.

———. "The Pythagorean Texts of the Hellenistic Period." *Acta Academiae Aboensis* 30 (1965): 1–266.

Thomas, J. A. C. *Textbook of Roman Law.* Amsterdam, 1976.

Torrance, T. F. "The Hermeneutics of Erasmus." In *Probing the Reformed Tradition: Historical Studies in Honor of Edward A. Downey, Jr.,* edited by E. A. McKee and B. G. Armstrong. Louisville, 1989.

Tracy, James D. "Against the 'Barbarians': The Young Erasmus and His Humanist Contemporaries." *Sixteenth Century Journal* 11 (1980): 3–22.

———. *Erasmus of the Low Countries.* Berkeley, 1996.

———. "The 1489 and 1494 Versions of Erasmus' Antibarbarorum Liber." *Humanistica Lovaniensia* 20 (1971): 81–120.

———. *The Politics of Erasmus: A Pacifist Intellectual and His Political Milieu.* Toronto, 1978.

Trinkaus, Charles. *The Poet as Philosopher: Petrarch and the Function of Renaissance Consciousness.* New Haven, 1979.

———. "Protagoras in the Renaissance: An Exploration." In *Philosophy and Humanism: Renaissance Essays in Honor of Paul Oskar Kristeller,* edited by Edward P. Mahoney. Leiden, 1976.

Trout, D. E. "Augustine at Cassiciacum: otium honestum and the Social Dimension of Conversion." *Vigiliae Christianae* 42 (1988): 132–46.

Van Bavel, T. J. "The Influence of Cicero's Ideal of Friendship on Augustine." In *Augustiniana Traiectina,* edited by J. den Boeft and J. van Oort. Paris, 1987.

Verheijen, Luc. *Saint Augustine's Monasticism in the Light of Acts 4.32–33.* Villanova, 1979.

Voegelin, Eric. *Plato.* Baton Rouge, 1966.

von Fritz, Kurt. *Pythagorean Politics in Southern Italy.* New York, 1940.

Vukmir, Mladen. "The roots of Anglo-American intellectual property law in Roman law." *IDEA: The Journal of Law and Technology* 32 (1992): 123–54.

Walterscheid, Edward C. "Inherent or Created Rights: Early Views on the Intellectual Property Clause." *Hamline Law Review* 19 (1995): 81–105.

Watson, Alan. *The Law of Property in the Later Roman Republic.* Oxford, 1968.

———. *Legal Transplants: An Approach to Comparative Law.* 2nd ed. Athens, Georgia, 1993.

———. *Roman Private Law around 200 B.C.* Edinburgh, 1971.

———. *Rome of the XII Tables.* Princeton, 1975.

Watson, Stephen H. *Tradition(s): Refiguring Community and Virtue in Classical German Thought.* Bloomington, 1994.

Weller, Barry L. "The Rhetoric of Friendship in Montaigne's *Essais.*" *New Literary History* 9 (1977/1978): 503–23.

Wilson, N. G. *From Byzantium to Italy: Greek Studies in the Italian Renaissance.* Baltimore, 1992.

Wood, Neal. *Cicero's Social and Political Thought.* Berkeley, 1988.

Woodmansee, Martha. "The genius and copyright: economic and legal conditions of the emergence of the 'author'." *Eighteenth-Century Studies* 17 (1983/84): 425–48.

Wootton, David. "Friendship Portrayed: A New Account of *Utopia*," *History Workshop Journal* 45 (1998): 29–47.

Zetzel, J. E. G. "Cicero and the Scipionic Circle." *Harvard Studies in Classical Philology* 76 (1972): 173–79.

Index

Adages, 31–32, 141, 142–48; as collected intellectual wealth of classical tradition, 25; and *philosophia Christi*, 28–29. "As we proceed the two of us along the way" (III.i.51): in the *Symposium*, 38; in the *Protagoras*, 60; "Do not break bread" (I.i.2), 135; "Do not sit on the grain measure" (I.i.2), 136; "Do not walk outside the public highway" (I.i.2), 136; "A friend is another self" (I.i.2), 135; "Friendship is equality" (I.i.2), 134; "Friends hold all things in common" (I.i.1), 4–5, 30–31, 91, 104, 109, 110, 116, 148–51, 158, 162–63, 164; in the *Laws*, 85; moved to first position, 25–26; in the *Phaedrus*, 67; in the *Republic*, 82; and the *Symposium*, 51; "The half is more than the whole" (I.ix.95), 110, 167; coupled with the opening adage, 27; on property, 27–28; "Know thyself" (I.iv.95), 57; "The labors of Hercules" (III.i.1), 3, 158–63, 170–73; "Like to like" (I.ii.21), 66; "Make haste slowly" (II.i.1), 143, 148, 151–58, 163, 171; "Nothing overmuch" (I.vi.96), 57; "Sacrificing

must be by odd numbers to the gods above, but by even numbers to the gods below" (I.i.2), 135; "The sileni of Alcibiades" (III.iii.1), 8–9, 26, 28, 30–31, 78, 167; on the philosophical life, 56; in the *Symposium*, 36; "Sparta is your portion; do your best for her" (II.v.1), 109–10; "Transgress not salt and trencher" (I.vi.10), 137; "Walk not in the public highway" (I.i.2), 135–36; "War is sweet to those who have not tried it" (IV.i.1), 165–69; "What have I done wrong" (III.x.1), 138

Adagiorum chiliades, Adages (1508), 1–7, 10, 142

Anachōrēsis (withdrawal): in Basil, 124

Antibarbarians, 10, 20–21, 24, attack on enemies of classical learning, 17–18; in form of Platonic dialogue, 17; on Pythagoras, 30; reading Augustine's *De doctrina*, 22–24; on spoiling the Egyptians, 22–24

Antisthenes, 8

Apostolic tradition, 14–15

Archytas, 119, 140

Aristotle, 90–92; against common property, 107–08, 168; cited in

Epictetus, 8–9
Equality. See *Isotēs*
Ercto non cito, 113–14

Francesco da Ravenna, Pier, 146
Froben, Johann, 2, 142, 149

Gaius, 11–12, 15; *Institutiones iuris civilis*, 11–12, 15
Gellius, Aulus, 122; cited in opening adage, 149; *Attic Nights*, 113–15
Gorgias, 46, 66
Gregory Nazianzus, 15

Hendrik van Bergen, Bishop of Cambrai, 24, 30
Hermans, William, 24
Hieroglyphs: and proverbs, 152–53
Horace, 160–63; *Ars Poetica*, 160–63

Iamblichus, 122, 128; on Pythagoras, 35–36; *De vita pythagorica*, 35–36, 41, 115–22
Institutio principis christiani, 110–11, 140
Isotēs (equality): and justice, 63–64; as opposite of *pleonexia*, 27, 63

Jerome, St., 33; on the *mulier captiva*, 18–19; on reading Paul, 18–20; as witness in *Antibarbarians*, 18; *Letters*, 170–73
Jesus Christ: compared to a silenus, 8; compared to Socrates, 26, 56; holding values similar to Plato, 27; like Plato and

Pythagoras, 29–31, 168; user of proverbs, 26
John the Baptist, 8
Justice, 165; as basis of friendship, 82; Cicero on Pythagoras as philosopher of, 97; divine and human in Aristotle, 92; in the *Gorgias*, 63; as *isotēs*, 63; as property transaction in the *Republic*, 80; in the *Republic*, 82

Kosmos: in the *Gorgias*, 64–65, 67; and the ordered life or *kosmios bios*, 65, 69; in Pythagoreanism, 64–65, 67

"Letter to Lambertus Grunnius" (Ep. 447), 138–40
"Letter to Paul Volz" (Ep. 858), 138

Mancipatio: in opposition to *traditio*, 11
Manuzio, Aldo, 142, 146–48, 152–58, 170
Meditation. See *Meletē*
Meletē (meditation), 140; as part of *askēsis*, 114–15; in Augustine, 130; in Basil, 123–25; and the philosophical life, 73–74; as distinct from *empeiria*, 74; in the *Gorgias*, 76; as opposite of *ameleia*, 73; in the *Phaedrus*, 73–74, 76; combined with *physis and epistēmē*, 74; in the *Symposium*, 50–51
More, Sir Thomas, 1
Mulier captiva, 24, 141; in *Enchiridion*, 21; as used by Jerome, 18–20; as used by Origen, 19–20